MOOSE MOUNTAIN

CHILDREN'S LEADER GUIDE

Group

Loveland, Colorado

group.com

Group resources actually work!

This Group resource incorporates our R.E.A.L. approach to ministry. It reinforces a growing friendship with Jesus, encourages long-term learning, and results in life transformation, because it's

Relational
Learner-to-learner interaction enhances learning and builds Christian friendships.

Experiential
What learners experience through discussion and action sticks with them up to 9 times longer than what they simply hear or read.

Applicable
The aim of Christian education is to equip learners to be both hearers and doers of God's Word.

Learner-based
Learners understand and retain more when the learning process takes into consideration how they learn best.

Moose Mountain: Children's Leader Guide
Copyright © 2008 Group Publishing, Inc.

Visit our website: **group.com**

Credits
Creative Development Editor: Amy Nappa
Senior Editor: Karl Leuthauser
Chief Creative Officer: Joani Schultz
Copy Editor: Jessica Broderick and Pam Shoup
Art Director: Josh Emrich and Andrea Filer
Print Production Artists: Lynn Gardner and Pam Clifford
Cover Art Director/Designer: Josh Emrich and Andrea Filer
Illustrators: Illustrated Alaskan Moose, Inc. and Josh Emrich
Production Manager: DeAnne Lear
Senior Project Manager: Pam Clifford
Senior Developer Children's: Patty Smith

Special thanks to Sara Tiedgen and her class: Alex, Alison, Ashley, Brian, Dalton, Daniel, Darby, Emily, Eric, George, Jaden, Kristen, Peter, Rachel A., Rachel B., Ricky, Rylee, and Travis.

Unless otherwise indicated, all Scripture quotations are taken from the Holy Bible, New Living Translation, copyright © 1996, 2004. Used by permission of Tyndale House Publishers, Inc., Wheaton, Illinois 60189. All rights reserved.

ISBN 978-0-7644-3825-7

10 9 8 7 6 5 4 3 2 1   15 14 13 12 11 10 09

Printed in the United States of America.

Contents

WELCOME TO MOOSE MOUNTAIN!

You're about to embark on an adventure.
Those who join you will never be the same.
Neither will you.

Moose Mountain makes a real difference in people who experience its life-transforming messages. These experiences affect the way they live. Your kids' time together will move them from just knowing about each other and Jesus to having a friendship with one another and God! These highly relational and experiential get-togethers promise to move any age from head knowledge to heart-transforming friendship. As your kids build friendships with one another, they'll find that Jesus is the best friend of all!

WHAT IS MOOSE MOUNTAIN?

It's a flexible, friendly, engaging 13-week series for small-group interaction that compares our friendships with others to our friendship with Jesus. At each get-together, children and leaders will…

• meet new friends in a fun, welcoming, non-threatening way;
• learn how friendships form;
• practice friendship skills; and
• discover and grow a friendship with Jesus.

Plus, you can get your whole church involved! Visit our Web site, www.group.com, to learn more!

WHERE CAN I USE MOOSE MOUNTAIN?

Moose Mountain works within your existing children's ministry program.

Great for classes!

If your program places children in classrooms based on their age or grade in school, you'll need one *Moose Mountain: Children's Leader Guide* for each classroom and one *Moose Mountain: For Kids* book for each child. Print a copy of this book for each child from the *Moose Mountain: For Kids* CD-Rom. Each Get-Together page is designed to be copied front-to-back.

Flexible for large group–small group format!

If your program follows a format where children and leaders gather first in a large-group setting and then move into small-group activities, you'll need one *Moose Mountain: Children's Leader Guide* for your large-group leader and one *Moose Mountain: For Kids* book for each child.

HEY, PARENTS!

Help your child introduce his or her friends to Jesus by using Moose Mountain in your home! Let your child invite several friends over for a weekly get-together, and guide kids through the activities in this book. Have a handful of kids in your home? Since Moose Mountain works for kids from kindergarten through fifth grade, you can let each child invite a couple of friends, and the whole family can be involved. You'll get to know your child's friends (and probably their families), see friendships bloom, and appreciate that kids are getting to know the best friend they could ever have—Jesus!

Easy for small groups!

No matter what your format is, be sure you (and other adult leaders) build relationships with the kids and get involved. Participate in games, Daily Challenges™, and sharing. Friends come in all shapes, sizes, and ages!

WHAT HAPPENS AT MOOSE MOUNTAIN?

During each get-together, kids will experience…

- **Wow!** As kids enter, they'll experience music, aromas, decorations, a project, or something else that will pique their curiosity and get them involved from the second they walk through the door.

- **What's New?** At this point, kids will get into their crews, and you'll guide them in reviewing how they've applied what they've learned so far and in sharing more about their lives.

- **Grins & Games**—Here kids join in an activity that lets them practice relationship-building skills in a bunch of fun ways!

- **Getting to Know Jesus**—This is where kids learn from the master of friendship: Jesus! They'll open their Bibles to discover what makes Jesus such a great friend.

- **Try It Out!** Here kids practice what they're learning with friends.

- **And more!** Since so many relationships are cultivated over meals, a delicious snack will be included in each get-together, as well as affirmations, music, Daily Challenges, and fun, fun, fun!

WHAT'S A DAILY CHALLENGE™?

Each week kids will complete Daily Challenges. These are specific ways children can put what they're learning into practice before your next get-together. Kids will find the Daily Challenges in their student books. Join in the adventure with kids and participate in the Daily Challenges, too! At each get-together, you'll celebrate the growth that happens through these Daily Challenges by having kids add to a colorful paper chain that will grow and loop around your room. The links remind us of friendship—a bond that continues on and on!

THE *Daily* CHALLENGE

> HI, FRIENDS! I'M ROOFUS THE MOOSE. I'LL BE POPPING IN WITH MY FRIEND ELLIE OWL TO GIVE YOU A FEW TIPS, OFFER FRIENDLY ADVICE, AND TELL A FEW JOKES.

> WE'RE GOING TO HAVE A LOT OF FUN TOGETHER!

WHAT DO I NEED?

You'll need this guide, one *Moose Mountain: For Kids* book for each child, one *Moose Mountain: Children's CD*, and the supplies listed in each get-together. If you have more than three crews (a crew is a leader and six kids), you might want to give each crew leader a *Moose Mountain: Children's Leader Guide* and let crews move through the get-together at their own pace.

HOW DO I GET STARTED?

Before your first Moose Mountain get-together, place each child into a crew. Each crew should have between six and eight members and a teen or adult leader.

Every child is vital. When a group gets bigger, it's too easy for someone to "disappear." Talkers dominate, and shy ones recede. Remember that each child has something to give. Each child has something to gain. Even Jesus limited his circle of friends to 12—and his closer circle only to three. If Jesus limited his scope of intimate friends, we can, too.

Depending on the size of your class or program, you'll have anywhere from one crew to 15 crews—or even more! Kids will stay in the same crew each week so they can really get to know each other and be comfortable sharing together. There's no special formula for creating crews. You might want to have crews that are all the same gender, or you could combine boys with girls. You might choose to group kids by the schools they attend, their interests, or their ages—or you might choose to mix everything up! Just be sure everyone has a crew, and then stick with your plan.

As you consider your facility, remember that the most important thing is for kids to be able to gather together comfortably. It's easiest to have kids circle up knee-to-knee on the floor for discussions so you can leave the room open for games and other activities. Or you can have kids gather around tables or move chairs into circles. Just be sure that they can see each other's faces and hear each other's voices as they talk—after all, eye contact and listening are key ingredients in building friendships!

HOW CAN I BE A GREAT MOOSE MOUNTAIN LEADER?

- Remember that Jesus loves children. Kids aren't objects or projects; they're real people. Even in the church, we can be guilty of viewing others not as real people but as notches in our Bible belt, or "projects" to bring around. No one likes to be seen as someone's project to "fix." It is God's Spirit of love that truly brings life change—and that happens as people see, hear, touch, and feel authentic faith lived through other people. This series allows children to discover the joys of friendship with others and Jesus.

- Be warm and hospitable. Moose Mountain requires relational leaders. You know the old saying: "To have a friend, you must be a friend." These get-togethers revolve around friendships. If you don't feel comfortable reaching out to others, join a group, but don't lead one.

- Be open. Be willing to honestly share your own life stories. To be transparent, you don't have to "disrobe"! Honest disclosure involves appropriateness. You can tell about past struggles without giving details that make children uncomfortable.

- Be willing to share the load. Find a co-leader, a friend who can partner with you to lead portions of the get-togethers. For example, the snacks often work best if handed off to someone who can concentrate on the food. Or designate someone to be the host to greet children on arrival. By sharing leadership, you're modeling working together as friends.

WHAT MAKES MOOSE MOUNTAIN UNIQUE?

- Food is an important part of Moose Mountain. Eating together creates special ties. Sharing food culturally is not just important today; it was important in Bible times as well. In the book *Many Tables*, Dennis E. Smith and Hal E. Taussig write, "The meal became the primary means for celebrating and enhancing community ties…'friendship' becomes especially associated with the bonds created at the table. In the New Testament, it is notable that Jesus is defined as a 'friend of tax collectors and sinners' precisely by his act of dining with them."

- We don't use the words "classes," "lessons," or "studies." Children and leaders join in "get-togethers." The purpose of Moose Mountain is to form friendships with others and God. It's intentionally not billed as an intense, information-filled Bible study. Instead, get-togethers are fun, safe opportunities for people to enjoy authentic relationships as they explore how God relates to people.

- Moose Mountain is designed specifically for small groups of six to eight people. This will encourage intimacy and deepening of people's relationships with each other and Jesus.

HOW DO I KNOW THAT MOOSE MOUNTAIN WORKS?

It really works! We know that because each get-together has been tested by real kids. Yes, real children from the real world have already experienced this. We've made the mistakes so you don't have to! To make it even easier, we've added insider tips as *"FIELD TEST FINDINGS"* to be your helpful friends along the way.

CREATING A CAMPY MOOSE MOUNTAIN

BUILD A FOREST

Use different sizes of artificial Christmas trees to create a fabulous forest. Spray some pine-scented air spray nearby to help kids imagine they're in the mountains. Place the trees around your room. Be sure to put some next to the log cabin and at the entrance of your space.

CONSTRUCT A LOG CABIN

Find a large cardboard appliance box, and set the box on the floor with the opening at the top. Tape the two opposite top flaps together to form a triangular roof. Tuck the other two flaps inside. Draw a door and windows, and cut them out using a craft knife. Cut only three sides of the door leaving one long side as the door's hinge. Use brown paint to draw log patterns on the cabin.

MAKE A CAMPFIRE

Use paper towel tubes to make logs, and stuff crumpled yellow, red, and orange tissue paper in and around them to create the flames of a campfire. Tuck a flashlight under the "logs." Enclose the faux fire with a few rocks, and you've got a campfire.

PITCH A TENT

If you have a tent or can borrow one, set it up near the campfire. Or visit a local camping store. Most sell inexpensive kids tents that instantly assemble with a flick of the wrist—no stakes required! You can also create a tent by draping sheets over a table. Ask kids to bring in sleeping bags to place inside the tent.

USE CAMPING GEAR

Place canteens, mess kits, lanterns, campstools, flashlights, and compasses around your space. If you don't have camping gear, see if you can borrow some. You can also buy camp gear from most large discount stores or from sporting goods stores. Be sure to check out your local army surplus stores for super deals, too.

PLAY NATURE SOUNDS

Bring the sounds of the outdoors inside to add ambiance to your campsite. Play a nature sounds CD to surround kids with the noises of insects, birds, and other critters.

DON'T FORGET!

Don't forget to use the Moose Mountain theme song each week! Start each session with the song, play it in the background during games and snacks, and then again as kids leave.

The more you play it, the more they'll learn and enjoy it!

GET-TOGETHER

1

Bible Point: **JESUS WANTS TO BE OUR BEST FRIEND.**

Key Verse: **ROMANS 8:39**

"No power in the sky above or in the earth below—indeed, nothing in all creation will ever be able to separate us from the love of God that is revealed in Christ Jesus our Lord."

HOLY BIBLE

Bible BACKGROUND
FOR LEADERS

MARY CHOOSES A RELATIONSHIP WITH JESUS.
Luke 10:38-42

This account brings us into the home of Mary and Martha, who appear to be close friends of Jesus. The story begins with Mary sitting at Jesus' feet and Martha in the kitchen, preparing a meal fit for their special guest.

We learn that Martha was concerned about what she felt was her obligation—providing food and comfort for Jesus. Martha may have been a widow and appears to have been the head of the household. Her sister Mary lived with her. Martha probably wanted to sit and listen to Jesus, too, but felt she must first get the meal ready.

"If only Mary would help," she probably thought, "we could both sit and listen to Jesus later." With this thought festering in her mind, Martha went to Jesus with a blistering accusation: Mary was loafing while she was doing all the work.

Jesus responded that Martha was worried and upset over the wrong things. Jesus wanted Martha to make a relationship with him her top priority, as Mary had done. Only one thing was truly important: spending time with Jesus, sitting at his feet and soaking in the truth he imparted so that she could live more fully for him.

Making It Personal

- Read John 11:17-44.
- What does this account reveal about Mary and Martha?
- Are you more like Mary or more like Martha?
- Pray: Dear God, help me to grow in my friendship with you. Help me to be more like Mary in the areas of…

MARY AND MARTHA

A Quick Overview

Activity	Kids will...	You'll need...
WOW!	Prepare for a surprise party.	Birthday party decorations, unfrosted cupcakes, frosting, plastic knives, wet wipes, decorating items, *Moose Mountain: Children's CD*, CD player, name tags
WHAT'S NEW?	Consider how they spend the hours of a week.	Tape measures
GRINS & GAMES	Play an introduction game.	Get-Together 1 page from *Moose Mountain: For Kids*, pens or pencils, *Moose Mountain: Children's CD*, CD player
Getting to Know JESUS	Discover that Jesus desires our friendship.	Gift boxes with removable lids, mirrors, Bibles, *Moose Mountain: Children's CD*, CD player
TRY IT OUT!	Practice asking get-to-know-you questions as they get to know each other better.	Party supplies from "Wow!" activity, optional game or party supplies, *Moose Mountain: Children's CD*, CD player
See You Soon	Choose a Daily Challenge to put what they've learned into practice.	Daily Challenges from Get-Together 1 page, pens or pencils, tape, scissors

MOOSE TRACKS

Bring along a noisemaker to each get-together. You can use it to get kids' attention after activities or discussions.

SUPPLIES & MATERIALS

You'll need name tags and birthday party decorations, such as streamers, balloons, tape, and confetti. And what's a party without food? You'll need unfrosted cupcakes, frosting, plastic knives, wet wipes, and lots of fun decorating items, such as sprinkles, candies, and colorful gels. Grab the *Moose Mountain: Children's CD* from your kit, and plug in a CD player.

GO ALL OUT!

Really wow your kids by covering the tables with colorful tablecloths (disposable ones work great!), hanging a "Happy Birthday!" banner from a party store, and providing birthday party hats—you know, the pointy kind with a little elastic strap. Be sure you wear one, too!

FIELD TEST FINDINGS

When kids saw all the cupcakes and party items, they started whispering to each other, "Whose birthday is it?" The anticipation in the room was high as kids wondered what we were doing and who was going to get to eat the food!

WOW!

Before kids arrive, hang just a few streamers or balloons, then spread the other decorating items on a table where kids can reach them. Turn on the CD player, and keep tracks 1-10 from the *Moose Mountain: Children's CD* playing as kids arrive. Put the cupcakes where kids can see them, but not where they'll get in the way of your other activities. You'll also need a name tag for each child. Kids will use the name tags to find their crews, so use stickers or colors to indicate the crews. For example, you might have all blue name tags for one crew, yellow for another, and so on.

As each child arrives, introduce yourself and say something like: **Hey! Glad you're here! We're having a surprise birthday party today, and I need your help!** Have children put on name tags, then get them immediately involved with decorating the room. Kids can hang streamers, blow up balloons, hand pieces of tape to the person hanging streamers, sprinkle confetti on tables, and so on. While you bustle about and encourage kids with their work, continue to mention the surprise birthday party and how you hope the guest of honor will feel special. If kids ask you who the party is for, just say it's someone very special.

MOOSE TRACKS

Calling kids by their names helps them feel special—use kids' names often!

ALLERGY ALERT

You'll see this icon each time children touch or eat food. Be aware that some children have food allergies that can be dangerous. Know your children, and consult with parents about allergies their children may have. Also be sure to carefully read food labels, as hidden ingredients may cause allergy-related problems.

WHAT'S NEW?

SUPPLIES & MATERIALS

You'll need one tape measure for each crew.

When everyone has arrived and your room is nicely decorated, turn off the CD, and gather kids together. **SAY: We'll get back to our surprise party soon, but right now I want to welcome each of you and tell you a little bit about what we'll be doing the next few weeks. We're going to be making friends, and as we make friends, we're going to see that ✝ Jesus wants to be our best friend! Each week you'll join with your crew for a bunch of fun experiences. So let's find out who's in each crew!**

Have children look for others who have similar name tags. Let kids know that they're supposed to look for people with name tags of the same color or with the same sticker, depending on your system. Explain that when they've found everyone in their crew, they should sit in a circle.

When everyone is sitting in a crew, give each crew a tape measure. **ASK: Who knows how many hours are in a day?** Let kids call out responses. **So if there are 24 hours in a day, how many hours are there in a week?** Those who are quick with math will call out 168 hours. **SAY: That's right! If we let one inch of our tape measure represent one hour, we'd need 168 inches.** Have each crew pull out 168 inches of tape from their tape measure.

MOOSE TRACKS

If you've got a lot of kids, this will take a little time. Turn this into a game by playing track 1 on the CD while kids mill about the room looking for their crew members.

ANYONE SEEN MY CREW?

THEY'RE OVER HERE. FOLLOW ME!

FIELD TEST FINDINGS

Kids love to play with tape measures! They had a great time pulling them out and snapping them back—and quickly caught on to the concept of measuring hours with inches.

One boy quickly called out, "Jesus is with us all the time!" and pulled his crew's tape measure as far as it would extend.

What's New? Continued...

ASK: How many of those inches do you think you spend sleeping? Let kids call out their responses, then **SAY:** Let's say that each of us sleeps eight hours each night. Over a week that would be 56 hours. Let's see what that looks like on our tape measures. Have crews measure 56 inches on their tape measures. **ASK:** What about school? How much time do you spend in school in a week? If you went to school seven hours a day, five days a week, how many hours would that be? When kids call out 35, have them measure 35 inches on their tape measures.

SAY: Now let's think about how much time we spend playing. That might be watching TV, playing sports, reading, hanging out with friends, or whatever is fun for you. Let kids call out the hours they estimate and show each other that many inches on their tape measures. **ASK:** How much time do you think you need to spend with someone to become friends with that person? Let kids call out times and show them in inches. **What if that person was your very best friend? Does that person get more time?** Let kids call out times and show them in inches. **What about time spent with Jesus?** Let kids call out how much time they think they spend with Jesus each week.

SAY: Some people only think about Jesus when they're at church. That would be only one hour a week! Have crews measure one inch. **That's a tiny amount of time.**  **Jesus wants to be our best friend. How can we get to know someone if we only spend an hour with that person each week? We're going to start learning ways to spend more time with Jesus and get to know him a lot better! And the whole time we're doing this, we're going to get to know each other better, too! Our get-togethers are all about friendship—so let's have some fun with our friends right now!**

Gather the tape measures.

GRINS & GAMES

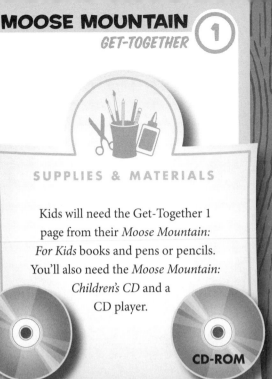

SUPPLIES & MATERIALS

Kids will need the Get-Together 1 page from their *Moose Mountain: For Kids* books and pens or pencils. You'll also need the *Moose Mountain: Children's CD* and a CD player.

CD-ROM

SAY: One of the first things we do when we meet someone is to introduce ourselves. Take turns introducing yourself and shaking hands with each person in your crew. Even if you've met someone in your crew before, say "Hi! My name is [insert your name]. It's nice to meet you!" Then shake hands with the person. Remember to be kind and friendly with your handshake.

Allow a few minutes for children to do this.

SAY: Another thing we do when we first meet people is to try to learn a little about them. Let's play a fun game that will help us learn more about our friends.

Have kids find the "You're a Fun Friend!" activity in their student books, and distribute pencils or pens. Explain that each child should find all the people in his or her crew who match the descriptions on the page and should write their names in those boxes. Kids can write their own names in the boxes as well so they can find out things they have in common with others. Play "I Will Be Your Friend" (track 1) on the CD as kids take time to learn about their friends.

If you have one crew, talk with kids about the things they have in common. If you have more than one crew, choose a few items from the handout, and have all those who answered these questions stand. For example, have all those who speak more than one language stand, then have those who like pizza stand, and so on. This will let children see how much others have in common with them. Then have children put their pages aside.

MOOSE TRACKS

If you have younger elementary students or children who are not reading yet, point out that each description has a picture beside it. Kids who don't read can figure out that the picture of the dog means "I have a dog" and so on. Even if children don't figure out the exact thing they're looking for, they'll still be talking to each other and making friends—and that's the whole point!

SUPPLIES & MATERIALS

You'll need a gift box with a removable lid and a mirror. Place the mirror inside the box so that when children lift the lid, they see their own reflection. If you have more than one crew, prepare one box for each. Add to the fun by playing tracks 1 and 2 on the *Moose Mountain: Children's CD*. If kids want to sing along, you can find the lyrics on page 172.

MOOSE TRACKS

If you have more than one crew, make sure crew leaders are clued in ahead of time about the mirrors inside the boxes. Have them pull each child aside to peek in the crew's box. If you have a lot of crews in one room, have the children sit facing away from the center of their circles, then let each child turn around one at a time to look into the crew's box.

CAN I TAKE A PEEK, TOO?

Getting to Know JESUS

ASK: **If Jesus was in your group, which boxes do you think he would have put his name in?** Let children share their responses with their crews. **SAY:** **We might not think of Jesus as hanging out with friends, but he spent a lot of time with his friends. The Bible tells of many times Jesus went on walks with friends, went fishing with friends, or just hung out talking with friends. We also know that he often ate with his friends.** Act as if you suddenly remembered the surprise party. **Ate? Oh my! I just realized that we've forgotten all about our surprise party!** Begin to act stressed about the party, and quickly begin questioning the kids, not really allowing them much time to respond. **ASK:** **Do you think everything is ready? Do you think our guest of honor will be surprised? Will our guest like the party? Will the food taste OK? Is it going to be fun? Did we forget anything? What might I have forgotten?** Then **SAY:** **I know! I forgot to tell you who the party's for! It's a big surprise, and it's for someone very special. I'll give each of you a clue, but you've got to keep it a secret!**

Invite each child to come up and look inside the box you've prepared. Make a big show of this being a surprise, and let kids know they shouldn't tell others who the party is for. When each child has had a turn, **ASK: Who is our party for?** The kids will respond with "Me!" or "Us!" **SAY: You're right! The party is for you! Surprise! Before we get started with the festivities, I want to tell you about a party Jesus was at. We can read about it in the Bible by turning to Luke 10:38-42—and we might learn something surprising about Jesus as we read!** Have children each find this passage in their Bible, then read it aloud or have one of the children read it aloud. **ASK:**

MOOSE TRACKS

As you ask the questions, have children discuss their thoughts with their crews instead of calling out their answers to the whole class. After each question, you can have a representative from two or three crews share an answer. This is one more way we make friends—by talking with them!

- **Jesus was the guest of honor at this party. Who was treating Jesus like a friend? How can you tell?**
- **How were Martha's actions like the way I was treating you as we got ready for the party?**
- **How did you feel when you didn't know who the party was for?**
- **How did you feel when you found out that the party was for you?**
- **What do you think Jesus meant when he said only "one thing" was needed?**

SAY: Jesus was the guest of honor, but Martha was so busy with preparations that she forgot to spend any time with Jesus! That's like when I was so busy worrying about our party that I forgot to tell you that the party is for you! We would never invite a friend over and then ignore the friend. Instead, we'd spend time with the friend and get to know that person better—and hopefully we'd have a lot of fun! ✝ **Jesus wants to be our best friend. What does that mean to you?**

Let children share their responses in their crews, then call on a few children to share with the entire group.

SAY: During the next few weeks, we'll learn more about what it means to have a friendship with Jesus. We'll learn how to be good friends from the example Jesus gave us, and we'll try out what we're learning as we grow in our friendships with each other. Let's put what we're learning today into practice by having fun with our friends at this surprise party!

SUPPLIES & MATERIALS

You'll need all the party supplies from the "Wow!" activity, along with any additional game or party supplies you decide to include based on the suggestions in this section. You'll also need the *Moose Mountain: Children's CD* and a CD player.

GO ALL OUT!

How about a piñata? Fill one with candy or inexpensive toys, and let children take turns trying to break it. When the loot spills, have everyone help gather it into one large bucket or bowl, and then divide the treats evenly among the children.

Party bags would make this an over-the-top event! Tuck a few trinkets or pieces of candy into a small bag for each child. That really says, "Wow! I'm glad you're my friend!"

TRY IT OUT!

ALLERGY ALERT
See page 12.

Let kids enjoy the party everyone's created! Bring out the cupcakes and decorating supplies, and let children decorate their own cupcakes. Be sure that kids clean their hands with wet wipes or at a nearby sink before and after handling food. Have everyone join in singing "Happy Birthday." If you'd like, let each child put a birthday candle on his or her cupcake, then light the candles and let children blow them out. Be sure there is plenty of adult supervision if you choose to light the candles.

Have children get their "You're a Fun Friend!" pages out again, and use them to play a new game. Turn on "Must Be Done in Love" (track 6) on the CD, and tell kids to mill about the room. When you stop the music, kids should each find one or two others who have similar answers in one of the boxes. For example, if a child has a dog, he or she might find one or two others who have dogs. When kids have each found one or two others with a similar interest or ability, they should sit down. When everyone is seated, kids should say to their partners, "Tell me more about_____" and fill in the blank as it relates to the area they have in common. For example, if two children both have dogs, one would say, "Tell me more about your dog. What's your dog's name?" or "What kind of dog do you have?" Allow a minute or two so each child gets to learn something about his or her partner. Then begin the music again, and play as time allows. Suggest that children find as many new partners as possible as you play.

When the game is over, **ASK:**
- **What are some interesting things you've learned about your friends here?**
- **How does having things in common help a friendship to grow?**
- **What things do you think you might have in common with Jesus?**
- **How could these things help you become better friends with Jesus?**

SAY: You have all just practiced something that's helpful when you make a new friend—learning more about that person and finding out what you have in common. We'll do things like this every time we get together so we can become better friends here and when we leave! You can use these friendship ideas anywhere—at home, at school, at sports, or at club activities.

See You Soon

SAY: When we were looking at the tape measures earlier, we thought about how much time it takes to have a friend. We all like to spend time with friends. But what could keep you *away* from time with your very best friend? Kids may say that homework, parents, or other responsibilities keep them from time with their friends. Guide children in discussing these questions with their crews:

• How do you feel when these things get in the way of your friendships?
• What keeps us away from time with Jesus?
• How do you feel about that?
• How do you think Jesus feels about that?

SAY: ✝ Jesus wants to be our best friend, and that takes time with Jesus. And even though we might not make time for Jesus each day, the Bible tells us that nothing, absolutely *nothing,* can get in the way of Jesus' love for us. 🗩 Romans 8:39 says, "No power in the sky above or in the earth below—indeed, nothing in all creation will ever be able to separate us from the love of God that is revealed in Christ Jesus our Lord." Nothing! How do you feel knowing that Jesus' love for you is so powerful? Let children share their thoughts in their crews.

It doesn't do us much good to just *know* that Jesus loves us and wants to be our best friend. We need to put what we're learning into practice when we leave this room. Each week we're going to pick a Daily Challenge. This is a fun way we can put what we're learning at our get-togethers into practice when we're at home or school—or wherever we are! Your Daily Challenges for this week are on the bottom of your student page. Go ahead and take them out.

Have each child cut out the Daily Challenge section of his or her student page. Read aloud the Daily Challenge options for this week, then have kids each choose and mark one option they're willing to commit to doing before your next get-together.

SUPPLIES & MATERIALS

Kids will need scissors, the Daily Challenge part of this week's student page, and pens or pencils. You'll also need a roll of tape.

MOOSE TRACKS

If you have younger children or nonreaders, take time to read the Daily Challenges out loud and help them choose one for the coming week. The ideas have pictures beside them to help even nonreaders understand their choices.

You can guide children in prayer by having them say, "Thank you for my friend _____" and letting them fill in the name of friends.

See You Soon Continued...

When each child has chosen an option, show kids how to wrap the Daily Challenges around their wrists and secure them with tape. Tell kids that they can take home the remaining portion of their student page and play the game with family members or other friends. They can complete the activity on the back side as well.

SAY: When you come back next week, we'll begin a project that will help us see how we're doing with our Daily Challenges. I can't wait to see you all next week! Getting together with you is fun as we all become better friends—with each other and with Jesus! Let's talk to Jesus now.

Encourage kids to turn their focus to God. If time permits, have the children share prayer needs with their crews and pray for one another.

Then close the time in prayer. Pray for the kids who are there, thanking God for loving them and for desiring a relationship with each child. Ask God to help the kids as they reach out to new friends and as they complete their Daily Challenges.

MORE TIME FOR FUN?

If you still have time, let kids work in their crews to complete the back side of their student page. Encourage kids to share their responses and thoughts with others in their crew. If kids don't have time to finish these reflections on the get-together, encourage them to take time at home this week to do so.

MOOSE MOUNTAIN

GET-TOGETHER

2

Bible Point: **JESUS SHOWS US HOW TO BE A FRIEND.**

Key Verse: **JOHN 15:12**

"Love each other in the same way I have loved you."

HOLY BIBLE

JESUS CALLS MATTHEW.

Matthew 9:9-13

To collect taxes in their vast empire, the Romans hired tax collectors from among the people over whom they ruled and allowed those tax collectors a great deal of freedom to tax people beyond what was required by Rome. Thus, tax collectors were often very rich men and also widely despised by the people they taxed. This is the class of people Matthew belonged to when Jesus called him.

At least two things about this event would have been a shock to onlookers. First, Matthew probably had a huge fortune and a lucrative business, and he didn't seem to bat an eye about leaving it all behind when Jesus called him. Something about Jesus kept Matthew from even thinking twice about all he stood to lose. The second big surprise would have been the actions of Jesus. For Matthew it probably seemed natural to throw a big bash and invite all his friends—many of them dishonest tax collectors—to meet his astounding friend. But for Jesus to actually attend this party was what stirred the ire of the Jewish leaders. By eating with such sinful people, who were ceremonially "unclean," Jesus was ignoring the standards that the leaders demanded all good Jews obey.

Jesus' response to the Pharisees' objections shows why Jesus identified with his new friend—he cared more about Matthew's eternal standing than about his own standing among the Jewish leaders. Jesus demonstrated to the Pharisees how to be a true friend.

Making It Personal

• Read Proverbs 18:24.
• What kind of friend are you? How could you be a better friend?
• Pray: Lord, thanks for being so much more than a friend to me.
  Help me be the friend you want me to be to...

A Quick Overview

Activity	Kids will...	You'll need...
WOW!	Inspect gift boxes to determine who might receive each gift and what the enclosed gift might be.	Several boxes of various sizes, various styles of wrapping paper, gift bows, tape, cookies or brownies, *Moose Mountain: Children's CD*, CD player
WHAT'S NEW?	Share how they completed their Daily Challenges, and add to the Friendship Chain.	Bright-colored construction paper, tape, scissors
GRINS & GAMES	Play a game that brings smiles and helps practice friend making.	
Getting to Know JESUS	Learn from Jesus' example how to get beyond first impressions.	Bibles, wet wipes, gifts boxes used in "Wow!" activity
TRY IT OUT!	Consider the first impression they make, and share what's inside them that others should know.	Get-Together 2 page from *Moose Mountain: For Kids*, pens or pencils, gift wrap, scissors, tape
See You Soon	Choose a Daily Challenge to put what they've learned into practice.	Daily Challenges from Get-Together 2 page, pens or pencils, tape, scissors

THIS IS EXCITING! LET'S GET STARTED...

SUPPLIES & MATERIALS

You'll need several boxes of various sizes. Boxes can be empty cereal boxes, shoe boxes, and so on. You'll also need enough cookies or brownies for the whole class, various styles of wrapping paper and bows, and tape. Grab the *Moose Mountain: Children's CD* and a CD player while you're at it!

Before kids arrive, wrap each box in wrapping paper that indicates a different occasion. Think of occasions such as birthdays for girls, birthdays for boys, anniversaries, baby showers, bridal showers, Father's Day and Mother's Day, Valentine's Day, Christmas, Easter, and so on. Choose wrapping paper that indicates the occasion and who will receive the gift. For example, a box wrapped in pink paper decorated with teddy

GO ALL OUT!

Have fun with the wrapping! You can prepare as many boxes or packages as you'd like to make a wide variety of impressions. Be creative with bows, or attach fun objects to the packages, such as small toys, kitchen utensils, or lightweight tools. You can even spray one or two boxes with fragrance. This will make the gifts even more specific for an intended recipient.

MOOSE TRACKS

bears and balloons is most likely for a little girl's birthday. Wrap the cookies or brownies in one box. Place the boxes around the room where kids are certain to notice them. Play tracks 1-10 on the *Moose Mountain: Children's CD* as children arrive.

When kids arrive, introduce yourself and say something like: **Hi! It's great to see you! I've got a bunch of presents here, and I wondered if you could figure out who they're for.** Encourage kids to examine the gift boxes. Ask them to think about who might receive each gift, what the occasion might be, and what they might find inside each box.

If you have a large number of children, you can make more than one of each style of box. Since the room will be busy with so many children, kids won't have a chance to inspect every box, so make a few of each, and spread them around.

If you have older elementary students, give them paper and pencils as they arrive, and let them write down their ideas about who would receive each gift and what would be inside.

If you have a large number of crews, wrap one box with cookies or brownies for each crew to make handing out food go more quickly.

SUPPLIES & MATERIALS

You'll need bright-colored construction paper, tape, and scissors.

GO ALL OUT!

Make your Friendship Chain wild, wacky, and super colorful! Choose gift wrap, neon-colored paper, or scrapbooking paper. You'll really decorate your room with fun!

When everyone has arrived, put the boxes aside. Have kids and leaders circle up with their crews, sitting knee-to-knee so conversation will be easier. Help those who weren't at the get-together last week to find their assigned crews. Give kids a chance to shake hands and introduce themselves to anyone new in their crews.

SAY: Last week we each chose a Daily Challenge to complete to show our friendship with Jesus. Let's take a minute or two now to see how that went!

Choose two or three kids or leaders to tell which Daily Challenge they picked and what happened when they carried it out. Then have everyone share in his or her crew so that each Daily Challenge is heard.

SAY: We want to celebrate the growth of our friendship with Jesus and with others, so each week we're going to add links to a Friendship Chain. How can a link in a chain remind you of friendship?

Let kids share their thoughts about the bonds of friendship, then demonstrate how to cut strips of paper and tape them into loops to form a chain. Younger children may need help with this, but older kids should be familiar with the concept. Have each child who completed a Daily Challenge last week add one link to the chain. If you have several crews, help them work together as they attach their last links so the chains from each crew are joined into one classroom chain. Then have leaders put aside the supplies and hold up the chain.

SAY: Wow! You've already shown the love and friendship of Jesus! Each week we'll add to this and see how many times we can go around our room—maybe we'll even make this long enough to go around the whole building! Now let's play a fun game that helps us practice making friends.

Tape the chain to a wall or someplace where children will be able to see it.

FIELD TEST FINDINGS

Every child and adult completed a Daily Challenge! The kids were excited about seeing a visual reminder of what they'd done.

MOOSE TRACKS

You can save time each week by pre-cutting strips of construction paper on a paper cutter.

ELLIE, WHAT DID YOU DO FOR YOUR DAILY CHALLENGE?

I HELPED MY NEIGHBOR CLEAN OUT HER NEST.

MOOSE TRACKS

Remind kids to use friendly handshakes and to not tickle the person they're trying to get to smile. Encourage them to give big smiles themselves to see if that will help the other person smile.

If you enjoy leading kids in singing, try "Your Friend" (track 10) on the *Moose Mountain: Children's CD*. Lyrics are on page 175.

GRINS & GAMES

If there are crews that have fewer than six members, let them join with another crew for this game. Have one person in each crew be the Friendmaker. Explain that the Friendmaker will go up to someone else in the crew, gently shake that person's hand, and say, "I want to be your friend. Will you please smile?" The person must respond by *not* smiling and by saying, "I want to be your friend, but I will not smile." If the person *does* smile, he or she becomes the new Friendmaker. If the person responds without smiling, the Friendmaker must move to a new person.

Play until each person has had a turn being the Friendmaker. Then have kids gather with their crews for discussion. **ASK:**

- **Was it easy or hard to be the Friendmaker? Why?**
- **Was it easy or hard to avoid smiling when the Friendmaker approached you? Why?**
- **Why is smiling so important when you first meet someone?**
- **What about shaking hands? Is that important? Why or why not?**

SAY: This game gave us a fun way to practice the first steps of friend making. When you first meet someone, you should look that person in the eyes, shake his or her hand, and smile. That helps us make a good first impression. Hey! Let's find out more about first impressions and what they're all about!

ALLERGY ALERT
See page 12.

SAY: You might be wondering why these gifts are all around the room. Hold up one of the gift boxes and **ASK:**

- Who is this a gift for?
- How can you tell?
- What do you think would be inside a box that's decorated like this?

Kids should easily figure out the occasion for the gift. Hold up several other boxes, and have kids answer the same questions. Then **SAY:** You were able to tell something about these boxes and even make guesses about what's inside each one based on the outside wrapping. That's called a first impression. What your eyes first see helps you form an idea in your mind. If you saw a present with Christmas trees on it, your first impression would be that it was a Christmas present. If you saw a pink gift with red hearts on the wrapping, your first impression would be that it was for Valentine's Day.

It's the same when we meet people. When we meet someone, we form a first impression. For example, you might see someone who is dressed in cool clothes and think, "That person must be really cool!" But you won't know if your first impression is correct until you get to know that person better. Let a child open one of the boxes that has cookies or brownies in it. **For example, you all thought this was a Christmas present** (or whatever kids thought it was depending on the wrapping). **But it's actually a present for you!**

If you have several boxes with cookies or brownies in them, let kids open these and distribute them. Be sure kids clean their hands with wet wipes or at a nearby sink before and after handling food. Let kids munch on their treats while you continue.

You'll need Bibles, wet wipes, and the gift boxes from the "Wow!" activity.

MOOSE TRACKS

You can add to the mystery of what's in each box by filling a few with items such as dried beans, an article of clothing, or a stuffed animal. Kids won't open these boxes, but if they shake them or pick them up, the boxes will have different weights or make different sounds.

FIELD TEST FINDINGS

We wrapped several boxes of packaged cupcakes and similar treats in a variety of papers. Kids thought the one with wedding gift wrap was probably a box of silverware. They determined that the box with antique cars on it was a tie for Father's Day, and they guessed that a pink box contained a doll. They were so surprised when they opened the gifts and discovered treats for them to enjoy!

MOOSE TRACKS

If you enjoy leading kids in singing, try "I Will Be Your Friend" (track 1) on the *Moose Mountain: Children's CD.* Lyrics are on page 172.

Getting to Know Jesus Continued...

SAY: Just as some of our boxes made the wrong first impression, people can get the wrong ideas about others from their first impressions. That person you met whom you thought was really cool? After you get to know that person, you might find out that he or she really is cool...or you might find out that he or she isn't someone you'd want to hang out with. Or you might meet someone and think, "No way will I ever be friends with him!" You might get to know that guy better and discover he's a great friend! **ASK:**

• **What would be your first impression if you met someone who looked like this?** Slouch your shoulders and frown for a moment, then let children share what their first impressions of you would be. Ask the same question a few more times, each time choosing a different expression or body position, such as crossing your arms and speaking like a drill sergeant, coughing and sneezing as you introduce yourself, talking very softly, turning your back, and so on. Really ham it up! The last time, give a friendly smile and extend your hand to one of the children as if you'd really enjoy getting to know that child. Then **ASK:**

• Why do you think first impressions are so important?
• When have you been wrong with a first impression?
• When have people been wrong in their first impressions of you? How does that feel?

SAY: Let's look in our Bibles to learn about a man who'd made a bad first impression, and let's see how Jesus treated him.

Have kids open their Bibles to Matthew 9:9-13. If you have older students, ask for a volunteer in each crew to read this passage aloud. If you have younger students, you can have your crew leaders read the passage to them.

SAY: Matthew was a tax collector. People didn't like tax collectors because they were known to be cheaters and they took money that didn't belong to them. A lot of people hated them! Imagine if you lived near Matthew. If you met him on the street one day, what might your first impression of him be? Show me your answer with your facial expression.

Let children respond, then **ASK:**

- What do you think Jesus' first impression of Matthew was? How can you tell?
- What did other people think of Matthew? What did they call him?
- What did Matthew do to show he wanted to be Jesus' friend?
- What did Jesus do to show he wanted to be Matthew's friend?

SAY: ✝ Jesus shows us how to be a friend. Jesus didn't care about first impressions. He could see that Matthew was a tax collector whom others didn't like. He could see that Matthew probably didn't have very many friends. But Jesus didn't let a first impression stop him. He asked Matthew to be one of his disciples—one of his closest friends! And then Matthew threw a party for Jesus! This made a lot of other people angry. They thought Matthew and the other tax collectors were scum! But Jesus knew Matthew and others like him needed a friend. So he took the first step and started a friendship with Matthew. We can be like Jesus and look past the first impressions others make to get to know the real person inside. Let's give this a try.

MOOSE TRACKS

Remember to have kids discuss their answers in their crews. This gives everyone a chance to share!

MY TURN! MY TURN! I WANT TO TALK, TOO!

SUPPLIES & MATERIALS

Kids will need the Get-Together 2 page from their *Moose Mountain: For Kids* books and pens or pencils. You'll also need a variety of gift wrap (bring along samples of all the kinds you used in the "Wow!" activity), scissors, and tape.

CD-ROM

MOOSE TRACKS

You can make this activity easier for younger children if you pre-cut the gift wrap into 5-inch squares.

If you have a large number of crews, give each crew a sampling of several different kinds of gift wrap so everyone has a choice.

FIELD TEST FINDINGS

One of the adult leaders was so impressed with how kids responded to this activity. She said, "Kids never get a chance to talk about these kinds of things! This is so good for them to be able to share like this."

TRY IT OUT!

SAY: Pick the kind of gift wrap that you think represents the first impression you make. For example, if others know you take ballet classes, you might pick pink paper. If you give a first impression that you're good at sports, you might pick paper with sporting equipment on it. If you give a first impression that you're a class clown, you might pick paper that has cartoon characters on it. Choose one of the kinds of paper, and cut it to fit over the box on your student page. Then tape the gift wrap along the top of the box so that it forms a flap. Show kids how to do this, then give them each time to choose gift wrap, cut it, and tape it onto the page.

When it appears that everyone is ready, **SAY:** Now lift up the flap of gift wrap, and write some good things about yourself that others might not know. These might be things that others can't tell from their first impression of you. Give an example from your own life, telling what others might think of you from their first impression based on your clothing or other physical qualities. Then share a good quality about yourself that others can't tell just by looking at you.

CAN I GET A LITTLE HELP HERE? I'M NOT TOO GOOD WITH SCISSORS!

After kids have had several minutes to work, have them circle up with their crews. **SAY:** Take turns showing others the gift wrap on the outside of your box. Tell what kind of first impression you think you make, and then show others what you've written or drawn under your gift wrap. Let others know some of the good things about you that go deeper than first impressions.

Allow time for children to share in their crews. You might want to remind children that this is a time of encouragement and a time to make positive comments. If someone shares something about himself or herself, it's not a time to make rude comments or laugh. Jesus shows us how to be friends, and his example is not a mean one.

When crews have had time to share, **ASK:**

- **What did you learn about someone in your crew?**
- **How did the things you learned help you get past the first impressions you had of others?**
- **Why do you think Jesus wants us to get to know one other beyond first impressions?**
- **Can you think of other ways** ✝ **Jesus shows us how to be a friend?**

SAY: ✝ Jesus shows us how to be a friend. He didn't care about the first impressions others had of Matthew. Jesus still reached out in friendship. And you know what's really amazing about this account? Matthew became one of Jesus' closest friends and even wrote part of the Bible! So Jesus really knew what he was doing by reaching out in friendship to Matthew. We can ignore the first impressions we've had of others and reach out in friendships too. And we can do our best to make a good first impression on others so they'll know right away that we love Jesus!

MOOSE TRACKS

If there are mostly younger children or those who don't yet write, let children draw pictures of good things that others might not know about them.

FIELD TEST FINDINGS

Some children were shy about sharing good things about themselves. Be encouraging and positive, and don't allow kids to make negative comments about themselves.

SUPPLIES & MATERIALS

Kids will need scissors, the Daily Challenge part of today's student page, and pens or pencils. You'll also need a roll of tape.

THE Daily CHALLENGE

MOOSE TRACKS

Encourage children to complete this sentence prayer: "Lord, help me be a friend to _____."

If you have younger children or nonreaders, take time to read the Daily Challenges out loud and help them choose one for the coming week. The ideas have pictures beside them to help even nonreaders understand their choices.

MORE TIME FOR FUN?

If you still have time, let kids work in their crews to complete the back side of their student page. Encourage kids to share their responses and thoughts with others in their crew. If kids don't have time to finish these reflections on the get-together, encourage them to take time at home this week to do so.

See You Soon

SAY: In John 15:12, Jesus tells us, "Love each other in the same way I have loved you." Jesus is telling us that we should follow his example of friendship. He loves us so much, and he wants us to show that love to others. It doesn't have to be a gigantic deal of giving presents and acting all mushy. It's as simple as smiling at someone and asking that person to sit with you at lunch. Let's see how we can put this verse, and the example of Jesus' life, into practice this week with our Daily Challenges.

Have each child cut out the Daily Challenge section of his or her student page. Read aloud the Daily Challenge options for this week, then have kids each choose and mark one option they're willing to commit to doing before your next get-together. When each child has chosen an option, show kids how to wrap their Daily Challenges around their wrists and secure them with tape. Tell kids that they can take home the remaining portion of their student page and talk to their families about first impressions. They can complete the activity on the back side of the page as well.

SAY: I'm so thankful that ✝ Jesus shows us how to be a friend. It helps me to have such a great example to follow. Now let's take time to talk to God about what's happening in the lives of our friends.

Have the children share prayer needs with their crews and pray for one another. Then close the time in prayer.

Pray for the kids who are there, thanking God for loving them and for desiring a relationship with each child. Ask God to help the kids as they reach out to new friends and as they complete their Daily Challenges.

CAN ANYONE TELL ME HOW TO READ THIS THING?

MOOSE MOUNTAIN

GET-TOGETHER

3

Bible Point: **JESUS ACCEPTS US.**

Key Verse: **1 JOHN 4:19**

"We love each other because he loved us first."

HOLY
BIBLE

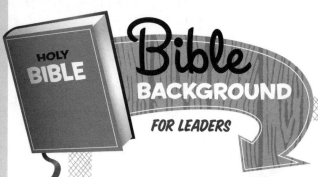

HOLY BIBLE

Bible BACKGROUND

FOR LEADERS

JESUS BEFRIENDS ZACCHAEUS.

Luke 19:1-10

Tax collectors are disliked today, but they were even more despised by the Jews of Jesus' day because they represented Roman oppression. Zacchaeus was not just a tax collector but a *chief* tax collector, which meant that he dealt and contracted directly with the Romans. This would have made him the richest and most despised of tax collectors. He would have been seen as a traitor and as someone who rejected the Hebrew faith and God. Few would have believed that Zacchaeus' sins could be forgiven.

It was not mere chance that Jesus looked away from the throngs of people who surrounded him and directly up into the tree at this seeker who wanted to see Jesus for himself. Zacchaeus didn't even have to say anything when Jesus spotted him; Jesus already had a plan for Zacchaeus.

Jesus' invitation to Zacchaeus surprised everyone. The people were stunned that Jesus would invite himself into the home of someone like Zacchaeus. Zacchaeus was stunned for the same reason! Everyone expected Jesus to keep himself pure from association with a sinner such as this tax collector. But Jesus wasn't concerned about people's errant expectations. He was concerned about drawing sinful people to faith in him.

Zacchaeus' decision to repay those he had cheated must have been a result of his trusting in God's grace—proof of a changed heart. Jesus' declaration that Zacchaeus had received salvation confirmed what had happened in Zacchaeus' heart. It also confirmed the fact that God would accept even a despised tax collector if he placed his faith in Jesus!

Making It Personal

- Read 1 John 4:19.
- Jesus took decisive action in reaching out to Zacchaeus, which resulted in Zacchaeus' joyful repentance. Who can you intentionally reach out to this week?
- Pray: Lord, thank you for reaching out to me. Help me reach out to…

A Quick Overview

Activity	Kids will...	You'll need...
WOW!	Create visual stories about themselves.	*Moose Mountain: Children's CD*, CD player, large sheets of newsprint, markers, tape, paper, pencils or pens
WHAT'S NEW?	Share how they completed their Daily Challenges, and continue the Friendship Chain.	Bright-colored construction paper, tape, scissors
GRINS & GAMES	Try to identify others just by seeing their feet or hands.	1 blanket for every 2 or 3 crews
Getting to Know **JESUS**	Act out the account of Jesus accepting Zacchaeus.	Bibles, *Moose Mountain: Children's CD*, CD player
TRY IT OUT!	Illustrate the book covers of their own life stories.	Get-Together 3 page from *Moose Mountain: For Kids*, markers or crayons, pens or pencils
See You Soon	Share the stories they created, and choose a Daily Challenge to put what they've learned into practice.	Daily Challenges from Get-Together 3 page, pens or pencils, scissors, stories kids created in "Wow!" activity, wet wipes, trail mix, napkins, roll of tape

SUPPLIES & MATERIALS

You'll need the *Moose Mountain: Children's CD,* a CD player, large sheets of newsprint, markers, tape, paper, and pencils or pens.

WOW!

Turn on the *Moose Mountain: Children's CD,* and play songs from tracks 1-10 while children arrive. This helps to create a fun and welcoming atmosphere!

As each child enters the room, invite him or her to begin creating a story about the people in his or her crew. As more people arrive, tell kids that they need to find ways to incorporate and include every crew member in the story. Encourage each crew to use the large sheets of newsprint and markers to create and illustrate its story. Suggest that everyone be involved, and provide pads of paper and pens so some can work on writing the story while others illustrate it. Let crews tape their stories to the walls as they complete them.

GO ALL OUT!

Without kids knowing, contact the parents of each child, and arrange to borrow a baby picture (or a color photocopy of a picture) of each child. Post these on the walls of your room. Let each child wander around and look for his or her own picture—as well as guess about the identity of others! Tie this in by reminding kids that these pictures represent the beginning of their stories and that Jesus is with us and loves us through each stage of our lives. This will take some planning, but it's worth it when you see the kids' responses!

FIELD TEST FINDINGS

The kids had a ball with this. They invented stories where they went to amusement parks, scaled volcanoes, and surfed in Hawaii. They loved creating adventures for themselves!

HEY, ELLIE, LET'S MAKE UP A STORY ABOUT OUR ADVENTURES TOGETHER! CAN YOU DRAW A PICTURE FOR OUR STORY?

SURE, ROOFUS! I'VE GOT A COMPUTER WITH ART SOFTWARE IN MY PURSE. LET ME GET IT OUT.

SUPPLIES & MATERIALS

You'll need bright-colored construction paper, tape, and scissors.

When everyone has arrived, put the stories and illustrations aside. Have kids and leaders circle up with their crews, sitting knee-to-knee so conversation will be easier. Help any newcomers find crews. Give kids a chance to shake hands and introduce themselves to anyone new in their crews.

SAY: Last week we each chose a Daily Challenge to complete to show our friendship with Jesus. Let's take a minute or two now to see how that went!

Choose two or three kids or leaders to tell which Daily Challenge they picked and what happened when they carried it out. Then have everyone share in his or her crew so that each Daily Challenge is heard.

SAY: We want to celebrate the growth of our friendship with Jesus and with others, so each week we're adding links to a Friendship Chain.

Point out the progress made on the Friendship Chain last week, then have each child who completed a Daily Challenge add one link to the chain. If you have several crews, help them work together as they attach their last links so the chains from each crew are joined into one chain. Then add this to the chain that was begun the first week. Have leaders put aside the supplies and hold up the chain.

SAY: Look at how you're spreading the love and friendship of Jesus! Now let's play a fun game that helps us get to know more about each other.

SUPPLIES & MATERIALS

You'll need one blanket for every two to three crews.

MOOSE TRACKS

If there are several crews, have two or three crews join together, and give each group a blanket. Let each group move to a different part of the room to play the game.

FIELD TEST FINDINGS

The kids really got into tricking each other by switching shoes, bracelets, and sweaters. The room erupted in laughter when a boy put on a girl's sandal and managed to trick everyone who recognized the sandal but not the foot!

GRINS & GAMES

Have two of your adult or teen leaders hold up the blanket in the front of the room. Choose three or four children to stand behind the blanket.

SAY: One person behind the blanket is going to stick out a foot or hand for us to see. You'll have to guess whose hand or foot it is!

Begin playing, letting kids make their guesses. When a child guesses correctly, that child can go behind the blanket and replace the child who just had his or her hand or foot displayed.

You can let kids try to trick each other by allowing them to switch shoes or take off their shoes behind the blanket. Be sure to encourage leaders to play, too! Play until each child has had a turn behind the blanket or as time allows. Then put away the blankets, and have kids circle up with their crews. Have them discuss these questions together:

- **What made this game hard? easy?**
- **How could you tell whose foot or hand was showing? What clues did you use?**
- **How does this game remind you of what we discussed last week about first impressions?**

SAY: We can sometimes identify people just by their hands or feet, and we can tell a few things about them by their hands or feet, too. But we can't really get to know people just by looking at them. We might know a little, but we don't know their whole story. We might accept or reject someone as a friend before we know that person's story. Let's check out the Bible to see what we can learn from Jesus' example.

MOOSE TRACKS

If you have a large meeting room, you might post the discussion questions on an overhead projector or on a PowerPoint system. This allows each group to remember the questions and move ahead in discussion at its own pace. Or provide each crew leader with his or her own *Moose Mountain: Children's Leader Guide.*

If you enjoy leading kids in singing, try "What a Friend We Have in Jesus" (track 2) on the *Moose Mountain: Children's CD.* Lyrics are on page 172.

CAN YOU TELL IT'S ME?

SUPPLIES & MATERIALS

You'll need Bibles, the *Moose Mountain: Children's CD*, and a CD player.

Getting to Know
JESUS

SAY: At our last get-together, we talked about first impressions and how Jesus looked past first impressions to become friends with a tax collector named Matthew. This week we're going to learn about another time Jesus reached out in friendship to someone others didn't like. This account helps us understand that 📖 Jesus accepts us. We can read it in our Bibles by turning to Luke 19:1-10, but I think it'll be fun if we act out this story.

Choose two volunteers to play the parts of Zacchaeus and Jesus and four or more people to be the crowd. Explain that you'll play the drama on the CD and the actors will simply do the actions suggested by the voices on the CD. Kids will need to listen closely for instructions—even those not chosen as actors will have a part.

Play "Short People in History" (track 11), and have everyone act along with the CD. Then have kids return to their crews and circle up for discussion. If you have older kids, suggest that they turn to Luke 19:1-10 and refer to this passage as they discuss the questions. If you have younger children, ask crew leaders to read the passage aloud before kids begin discussion. **ASK:**

• What did Jesus know about Zacchaeus?
• How did Jesus treat Zacchaeus?
• What did Jesus do to show that he accepted Zacchaeus?
• What did others do to show that they did not accept Zacchaeus?

SAY: Jesus knew all about Zacchaeus. He didn't know just a tiny bit of his life—he knew everything Zacchaeus had done. He knew Zacchaeus' whole life story, and he still accepted Zacchaeus. 📖 Jesus accepts us, too. He knows our whole life story—not just a tiny part—and he accepts us and offers us his friendship. And because 📖 Jesus accepts us, it makes us want to be better friends to others, just as Zacchaeus wanted to be a better friend and give back what he'd taken and more!

Let's dig a little deeper into this idea of accepting others as Jesus does.

TRY IT OUT!

SAY: Think about your own story so far—the part of your life that you know. Imagine that this page is the cover of the book that will tell the story of your life. You know your story so far. Others know little bits of it. Jesus knows all of it!

Be sure kids put their names on the covers, then have them use words or illustrations to personalize their book covers. Encourage kids to think about their interests, hobbies, families, pets, and so on as they make their book covers.

After 5 to 10 minutes, have everyone put aside the art supplies and form pairs. Ask children and leaders to share with each other about their book covers and what is represented on them. After several minutes, ask partners to discuss this question:

• **What do you think will happen in the upcoming pages of your life story?**

After a few minutes, have crews circle up and discuss these questions together:

• **People can accept us or reject us even though they only know part of our life story. What does acceptance look like? sound like? feel like?**
• **How do you feel knowing that Jesus knows your whole life story and ✝ he accepts you?**
• **How can you follow Jesus' example and reach out to others with acceptance? How can you do this at home? at school?**

SAY: Jesus is the best friend we could ever have, and ✝ Jesus accepts us, even when others don't. Look at the cover of your "life story" book, and find our verse, ❤ 1 John 4:19. Wait a moment for children to find this. **Let's say this together.**

Lead kids in saying, "We love each other because he loved us first." **ASK:** How can understanding this verse help us to accept others?

SAY: Let's set aside our own stories for a moment and look at the creative stories you put together earlier.

MOOSE TRACKS

If you have mostly nonreaders, say the verse aloud first, then have children say it with you a couple of times.

ALLERGY ALERT
See page 12.

SUPPLIES & MATERIALS

THE *Daily* CHALLENGE

Kids will need scissors, the Daily Challenge part of this week's student page, and pens or pencils. You'll also need the stories kids created in the "Wow!" activity, wet wipes, trail mix, napkins, and a roll of tape.

MOOSE TRACKS

You can make your own trail mix by stirring together all kinds of fun treats, such as mini pretzels, cheese crackers, raisins, Skittles candies, and so on. Yum!

If you have younger children or nonreaders, take time to read the Daily Challenges out loud and help them choose one for the coming week. The ideas have pictures beside them to help even nonreaders understand their choices.

Let kids share the stories they created in the "Wow!" activity. Have kids clean their hands with wet wipes or at a nearby sink, and provide trail mix for everyone to enjoy as they check out the stories they worked together to create.

When the story sharing is complete, **SAY:** It's fun to see and celebrate the stories you created. Every day, you are creating the story of your life. And no matter where that story takes you, Jesus will be there accepting you and offering you his friendship. ✝ Jesus accepts us and shows us how to accept others—no matter what their life stories are like. Let's look at our Daily Challenges. Choose one that will help you show that you accept someone this week.

Have each child cut out the Daily Challenge section of his or her student page. Read aloud the Daily Challenge options for this week, then have kids each choose and mark one option they're willing to commit to doing before your next get-together. When each child has chosen an option, show kids how to wrap their Daily Challenges around their wrists and secure them with tape.

SAY: I'm so thankful that ✝ Jesus accepts us. It helps me to have such a great example to follow. Now let's take time to talk to God about what's happening in the lives of our friends.

Have the children share prayer needs with their crews and pray for one another. Then close the time in prayer.

Pray for the kids who are there, thanking God for accepting them and for desiring a relationship with each child. Ask God to help the kids as they demonstrate acceptance to others and as they complete their Daily Challenges.

MORE TIME FOR FUN?

If you still have time, let kids work in their crews to complete the back side of their student page. This week they'll find it on the other side of their "life story" book covers. Encourage kids to share their responses and thoughts with others in their crews. If kids don't have time to finish these reflections on the get-together, encourage them to take time at home this week to do so.

MOOSE TRACKS

You can have children complete this sentence prayer: "Jesus, help me to accept _____." Have them each fill in the name of someone they'd like to know better.

THAT STORY WE MADE UP ABOUT GOING FISHING TOGETHER WAS PRETTY FUNNY. I LAUGHED MY ANTLERS OFF!

DID YOU LIKE MY ILLUSTRATIONS? I'M SURE TO WIN AWARDS FOR THOSE!

MOOSE MOUNTAIN

GET-TOGETHER

4

Bible Point: **JESUS IS KIND.**

Key Verse: **EPHESIANS 4:32A**

"Be kind to each other."

JESUS TOUCHES THE LEPER.

Matthew 8:1-3

During Bible times, there was no known cure for leprosy. If a priest declared that a person was infected with a contagious form of leprosy, that person was banished from his or her home and forced to live outside the city. Lepers could only live in communities with others like themselves, and they were required to call out a warning of "Unclean! Unclean!" to approaching travelers who might unknowingly come into contact with them. We can only imagine how devastating it was to be ostracized from others with such severity.

When Jesus encountered the leper, a higher purpose once again took precedence over the rules of society. Jesus was more concerned about the man's health and spiritual well-being than he was about the rules. Jesus didn't need to touch the leper to heal him (see Luke 17:12-14), but he did. In doing so, Jesus not only showed that he was powerful enough and cared enough to heal the man but also that he was kind enough to touch the man, who, because of his illness, may not have experienced human touch in many years.

Making It Personal

- Read Colossians 3:12.
- Would others describe you as kind? How can your relationship with Jesus prompt you to soften the moments when you tend to be harsh?
- God, help my kindness shine through to others, especially when I…

A Quick Overview

Activity	Kids will...	You'll need...
WOW!	See a disgusting "decoration."	Kitty litter brownies
WHAT'S NEW?	Share how they completed their Daily Challenges, and add to the Friendship Chain.	*Moose Mountain: Children's CD*, CD player, bright-colored construction paper, tape, scissors
GRINS & GAMES	Play a game that brings smiles and practices friend making.	Attention-getting device
Getting to Know JESUS	Compare their response to the snack to the response people had to the man with leprosy.	Bibles, kitty litter brownies from "Wow!" activity, wet wipes
TRY IT OUT!	Affirm one another with words of kindness.	*Moose Mountain: Children's CD*, CD player, self-adhering elastic bandages, scissors
See You Soon	Choose a Daily Challenge to put what they've learned into practice.	Get-Together 4 page from *Moose Mountain: For Kids*, pens or pencils, tape, scissors

SUPPLIES & MATERIALS

You'll need the ingredients and supplies to make brownies, and you'll need a box of Grape-Nuts cereal.

WOW!

Before kids arrive, make a batch of brownies using a favorite recipe or a boxed mix. Cook the brownies according to the directions in your recipe or on the packaging. While the brownies are still warm (but not too hot to touch), scoop a portion into your hands, and mold this into the shape of cat poop. (There's just no nice way to say that!) Then drop the molded piece of brownie into a pan of Grape-Nuts cereal. Do this with the rest of the brownies. The result is a tray of brownies that looks just like used kitty litter.

Place the kitty litter brownies on a table where kids will see them as soon as they walk through the door. There are sure to be gross-out comments, but you can just smile and indicate that the kitty litter is part of the surprise in today's get-together. Don't let on that it's really brownies—keep that under wraps for now.

While kids are discussing this unusual attention-getter, ask them questions about other things that seem disgusting to them. Kids will have plenty of stories about things they've seen, heard about, or smelled that were of an unpleasant nature.

MOOSE TRACKS

If you don't have time to make brownies, get the same effect by tearing and gently molding large Tootsie Roll candies.

FIELD TEST FINDINGS

We went all out to make these brownies look "realistic." When kids entered the room, there were plenty of wrinkled noses, raised eyebrows, and questioning looks!

GO ALL OUT!

Make the kitty litter effect complete by purchasing a new kitty litter box and scoop and placing the Grape-Nuts cereal and brownies in this. Even though you'll be using brand-new items, make sure they've been thoroughly washed before putting food items into them.

MOOSE TRACKS

Yes, this looks totally gross. Kids will love it! And it certainly helps today's kids understand how revolting a person with leprosy appeared back in Bible times.

WHAT'S NEW?

When everyone has arrived, put the kitty litter brownies aside. Have kids and leaders circle up with their crews, sitting knee-to-knee so conversation will be easier. Help any newcomers find crews. Give kids a chance to shake hands and introduce themselves to anyone new in the crews.

SAY: Last week we each chose a Daily Challenge to complete to show our friendship with Jesus. Let's take a minute or two now to see how that went!

Choose two or three kids or leaders to tell which Daily Challenge they picked and what happened when they carried it out. Then have everyone share in his or her crew so each Daily Challenge is heard. Play tracks 9-10 on the *Moose Mountain: Children's CD* while crews talk.

SAY: We want to celebrate the growth of our friendship with Jesus and with others, so each week we're adding links to a Friendship Chain.

Point out the progress made on the Friendship Chain last week, then have each child who completed a Daily Challenge add one link to the chain. If you have several crews, help them work together as they attach their last links so the chains from each crew are joined into one chain. Then add this to the big Friendship Chain. Turn off the music, have leaders put aside the supplies, and hold up the chain.

SAY: Look at how you're spreading the love and friendship of Jesus! Now let's play a fun game that helps us get to know more about each other.

SUPPLIES & MATERIALS

You'll need the *Moose Mountain: Children's CD,* a CD player, bright-colored construction paper, tape, and scissors.

SUPPLIES & MATERIALS

This game is noisy, so you'll need a loud attention-getting device, such as a whistle. Or you can flip the lights off and on to get kids' attention.

MOOSE TRACKS

If you have more than two crews, have kids form circles of two crews each to play this game. This will keep smaller kids from getting squished by bigger ones.

This game is a loud and rowdy one. If your classroom has desks or tables, move them aside. Or play this game outdoors.

Have everyone stand in a circle. **SAY: I'm going to call out describing qualities. If what I call out describes you, quickly move to the middle of the circle and link elbows with those who are like you to make a smaller circle. If what I say does *not* describe you, try to crawl or squeeze between those who have linked elbows and get into the center of that circle. For example, if I say, "Everyone wearing red" and you're wearing red, you'll move to the middle and link elbows with the others wearing red.** Have everyone wearing red do this. **Then those who are not wearing red will try to get into the middle of that circle. The people wearing red will squeeze close together to keep them out.** Have those not wearing red try to squeeze in now so everyone understands how to play the game. Then demonstrate your attention-getting device. Explain that kids should immediately freeze in place and stop speaking as soon as they hear it. Practice this once or twice so kids know what you expect.

Begin the game, calling out a variety of qualities or characteristics so everyone has a turn being included in the circle and everyone has a chance to be excluded from the circle. Here are suggestions for what you might call:

Everyone…

- wearing purple
- who has a dog
- who has more than one brother or sister
- who likes spaghetti
- who has been on an airplane
- wearing sandals
- who has a hamster

After each round, use your attention-getting signal, and have kids return to the larger circle for the next round. Then have everyone return to their crews to discuss these questions:

• **How did you feel when you were included in the inner circle?**
• **How did you feel when you were not included?**
• **When have you felt "not included" in real life? Share how that feels.**
• **When have you not included others? How do you think they felt?**

SAY: The Bible tells us about a group of people who were never included. They must have felt a lot like you did when you were left out in this game. Let's find out more!

GO ALL OUT!

There's a clip from the movie *Dumbo* that illustrates rejection in a way kids can relate to. It's about 9 minutes and 40 seconds into the movie and begins when elephants gather around Mrs. Jumbo to see her new baby. It ends when Mrs. Jumbo closes the window on the laughing elephants. Preview the clip and cue the movie to the correct place, then show this to kids before you move into the Bible story. *

* In general, federal copyright laws do not allow you to use videos or DVDs (even ones you own) for any purpose other than home viewing. Though some exceptions allow for the use of short segments of copyrighted material for educational purposes, it's best to be on the safe side. Your church can obtain a license from the Motion Picture Licensing Corporation for a small fee. Just visit www.mplc.com or call 1-800-462-8855 for more information. When using a movie that is not covered by the license, we recommend directly contacting the movie studio to seek permission for use of the clip.

I'M GLAD I WAS INCLUDED WITH FRIENDS WHO LIKE SPAGHETTI...

I DON'T LIKE SPAGHETTI, BUT I GOT TO BE INCLUDED WITH FRIENDS WHO HAVE HAMSTERS. I KEEP MINE IN A CAGE IN MY PURSE.

SUPPLIES & MATERIALS

You'll need Bibles, the kitty litter brownies, and wet wipes.

FIELD TEST FINDINGS

During this get-together, one boy felt comfortable enough to disclose to others that he had diabetes, and a girl shared that her mother had just been diagnosed with breast cancer. The kids were able to relate their own experiences to those of the lepers.

Getting to Know **JESUS**

ALLERGY ALERT
See page 12.

ASK:

• What's the worst disease you've ever heard of?
• If one of your friends got this disease, what would you do?
• Would you still be able to be friends?

SAY: In Bible times, there was a disease everyone dreaded called leprosy. People can still get leprosy today, but now there are ways to treat this condition. But in Bible times, there was no way to treat leprosy, so if you got this disease, you had to leave your family and friends and go live outside of town. You couldn't talk to others or get close to them because you might infect them. **ASK:**

• How do you think it would feel to discover that you had leprosy?
• How do you think it would feel to find out that one of your family members or friends had leprosy?

As you listen to the responses, walk over to the kitty litter brownies. Carefully select one, sniff it, and bite into it while kids are watching. They're certain to cry out in disgust or start a ruckus of laughter. Try to remain calm with an innocent expression as you respond.

SAY: What? You think what I'm eating is gross? That's probably how people felt about lepers back in Jesus' day. They were gross, and no one wanted to touch them or even get near them. But I've got a surprise for you! This isn't what you think it is! I'm actually eating brownies rolled in Grape-Nuts cereal. Do you want some?

Have kids clean their hands at a nearby sink or with wet wipes, then let those who dare select a brownie and eat it. It's likely that most kids will quickly overcome their aversion to the food and will join in this wild experience. When everyone who wants a brownie has had one, have kids circle up with their crews and read Matthew 8:1-3 together. If you have crews with younger children or nonreaders, have the crew leaders read the passage aloud. Then ask crews to tell you what happened in their own words.

After kids have retold the account, **ASK:**

- **What might the man with leprosy have been thinking when he saw Jesus coming near?**
- **What do you think Jesus thought when he saw the man with leprosy nearby?**
- **Everyone else thought the man with leprosy was disgusting and gross, but Jesus touched him. Why?**

SAY: We thought the brownies were gross before we knew what they really were. Then we were willing to accept them as food. Jesus showed his acceptance of the man with leprosy by showing kindness. ✝ Jesus is kind, and he chose to show kindness with a touch. **ASK:**

- **When have you felt like others didn't want to touch you or be around you? What was that like?**
- **Why does kindness matter in a friendship?**
- **What are examples of kindness?**

SAY: Let's do an activity to help us consider how we can be kind to others as Jesus was.

FIELD TEST FINDINGS

When our leader bit into a kitty litter brownie, the room erupted with laughter and "Gross!" comments. The kids loved it! When we offered them brownies, they quickly joined in eating—but they were commenting on the appearance the whole time. Interestingly enough, not many adults were willing to try the brownies!

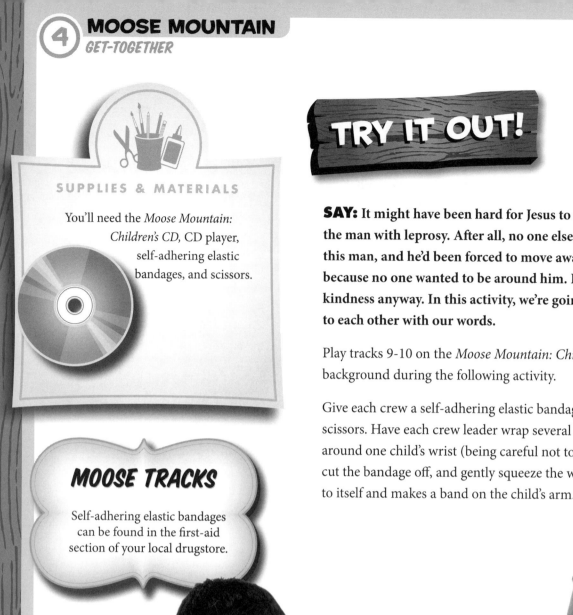

SUPPLIES & MATERIALS

You'll need the *Moose Mountain: Children's CD,* CD player, self-adhering elastic bandages, and scissors.

MOOSE TRACKS

Self-adhering elastic bandages can be found in the first-aid section of your local drugstore.

TRY IT OUT!

SAY: It might have been hard for Jesus to reach out and touch the man with leprosy. After all, no one else wanted to touch this man, and he'd been forced to move away from his home because no one wanted to be around him. But Jesus showed kindness anyway. In this activity, we're going to show kindness to each other with our words.

Play tracks 9-10 on the *Moose Mountain: Children's CD* in the background during the following activity.

Give each crew a self-adhering elastic bandage roll and a pair of scissors. Have each crew leader wrap several inches of bandage around one child's wrist (being careful not to wrap too tightly), cut the bandage off, and gently squeeze the wrap so it sticks to itself and makes a band on the child's arm. Have each crew

leader then look the child in the eyes and **SAY:** "[Child's name], when you see this bandage, remember that I think you're…" Have crew leaders complete the sentence with an affirmation. Encourage the other children in each crew to add other comments of affirmation, saying reasons why they like this child or why they're glad he or she is their friend. After everyone has had a chance to share, have each crew leader move to the next child and repeat the activity. Continue until each child has had a turn being affirmed with words of kindness.

After each child has been affirmed, **SAY:** Ephesians 4:32 in the Bible says, "Be kind to each other." Kindness is part of God's plan for friendship, and the words you've spoken to each other are a great way to express kindness. **ASK:**

- How do you feel when others are kind to you?
- What would it be like to choose to show kindness in your home? to your friends?
- How would your actions of kindness make a difference in the lives of others?

SAY: Let's get our Daily Challenges ready to make sure we show kindness!

FIELD TEST FINDINGS

We noticed that it was difficult for elementary boys to affirm girls in their crews, and girls didn't want to affirm the boys. Don't force anyone to share, but do encourage kids to express words of kindness.

MOOSE TRACKS

If you enjoy leading kids in singing, try "Your Friend" (track 10) on the *Moose Mountain: Children's CD.* Lyrics are on page 175.

I WONDER HOW I'M GOING TO GET OUT OF THIS ONE. THIS SELF-ADHERING BANDAGE REALLY ADHERES TO MY FUR. HELP!

SUPPLIES & MATERIALS

Kids will need scissors, the "Kindness Quiz" and Daily Challenge parts of the Get-Together 4 student page, and pens or pencils. You'll also need a roll of tape.

THE Daily CHALLENGE

MOOSE TRACKS

If you have younger children or nonreaders, take time to read the Daily Challenges out loud and help them choose one for the coming week. The ideas have pictures beside them to help even nonreaders understand their choices.

Encourage children to complete this sentence prayer: "Lord, help me show kindness to _____ this week."

MORE TIME FOR FUN?

If you still have time, let kids work in their crews to complete the remaining sections of their student page. Encourage kids to share their responses and thoughts with others in their crews. If kids don't have time to finish these reflections on the get-together, encourage them to take time at home this week to do so.

See You Soon

Have each child cut out the Daily Challenge section of his or her student page. Read aloud the Daily Challenge options for this week, then have kids each choose and mark one option they're willing to commit to doing before your next get-together. When each child has chosen an option, show kids how to wrap their Daily Challenges around their wrists and secure them with tape. Encourage kids to wrap these around the wrists that don't already have bandages on them.

Then have kids look at the "Kindness Quiz" section of their student page. As a group or in crews, brainstorm specific ways kids can show kindness in each location or to each person. Help kids think of realistic things they can do, such as take a snack to the coach of their team, make a card for a teacher, smile and participate in class, let a brother or sister go first or have the largest piece of dessert, turn down the stereo so neighbors aren't disturbed, and so on.

SAY: This week you have your Daily Challenge to accomplish, but I'm going to challenge each of you to go even further with kindness this week. See if you can really go wild with kindness in as many ways as possible!

I'm so thankful that ✝ Jesus is kind. It helps me to have such a great example to follow. Now let's take time to talk to God about what's happening in the lives of our friends.

Have the children share prayer needs with their crews and pray for each other. Then close the time in prayer.

Pray for the kids who are there, thanking God for being kind to them and for desiring a relationship with each child. Ask God to help the kids as they demonstrate kindness to others and as they complete their Daily Challenges.

MOOSE MOUNTAIN

GET-TOGETHER

5

Bible Point: **JESUS LISTENS TO US.**

Key Verse: **EPHESIANS 4:29B**

"Let everything you say be good and helpful, so that your words will be an encouragement to those who hear them."

JESUS BLESSES THE CHILDREN.

Mark 10:13-16

In this passage, some parents have brought their children to be touched and blessed by Jesus. But the disciples, apparently thinking it is their job to protect Jesus from the masses (especially those as insignificant as children), turn these families away. Jesus surprises his followers not only by rebuking his disciples for their actions but also by welcoming the children into his arms.

If you were the parent of one of those small children whom the famous Jesus of Nazareth stopped to bless, what would *you* think of Jesus? How would you respond later when you heard he'd been crucified and then rose from the dead? If you were one of the children, think about all the times you'd hear the story of being held and blessed by Jesus! Through this act of blessing the children, Jesus showed the common person—even the small child—how important we all are to him. He takes time to touch, bless, and hear us.

Another theme also winds though this passage: To make it to heaven, you must become like one of these small children. What did Jesus mean by that? What makes one fit for God's kingdom? The religious leaders had it all wrong. As the church sometimes does today, they relegated children to a place of insignificance until they grew to adults. Instead, we must value and encourage the qualities of children that make them receptive to the grace Jesus offers.

Your students are important to God, regardless of their age or influence. Help them see the mercy, grace, and friendship God offers in Jesus to every person everywhere.

Making It Personal

- Read Ephesians 4:29.
- Do the words children hear you speak bring encouragement to them? How could you improve in this?
- Pray: Lord, thank you for offering friendship to people of all ages. Help me to speak words of friendship and encouragement to…

A Quick Overview

Activity	Kids will...	You'll need...
WOW!	Try to identify songs and sound effects.	Get-Together 5 page from *Moose Mountain: For Kids*, pens or pencils, *Moose Mountain: Children's CD*, CD player
WHAT'S NEW?	Share how they completed their Daily Challenges, and add to the Friendship Chain.	Bright-colored construction paper, tape, scissors
GRINS & GAMES	Play a game that brings smiles and practices friend making.	Blindfolds, *Moose Mountain: Children's CD*, CD player
Getting to Know JESUS	Eat a snack that illustrates the story of Jesus blessing the children.	Round crackers, cheese spread, paper plates, wet wipes, plastic knives, assortment of chopped vegetables and grated cheese, Bible
TRY IT OUT!	Practice hearing and saying kind words about one another.	Paper, pens or pencils, tape
See You Soon	Choose a Daily Challenge to put what they've learned into practice.	Daily Challenges from Get-Together 5 page, pens or pencils, tape, scissors

THIS IS GOING TO BE SO MUCH FUN!

SUPPLIES & MATERIALS

Kids will need the Get-Together 5 page from their *Moose Mountain: For Kids* books and pens or pencils. You'll also need the *Moose Mountain: Children's CD* and a CD player.

CD-ROM

As kids arrive, give them their student page and play "What's That?" (track 12) on the *Moose Mountain: Children's CD*. Let kids use the clues on their student page to identify the sounds and songs. The clues are not in the same order as the sounds, so kids will want to work together and listen carefully to figure them out. Play the track again as time permits.

GO ALL OUT!

Place a few tape recorders around your room. As kids arrive, let them take turns recording jokes or talking while trying to disguise their voices. Later on, you can play the recording and see if kids can guess who's speaking. Kids love to hear their voices on tape—and it's fun to see how well we can recognize others' voices.

FIELD TEST FINDINGS

Kids in our field test had fun introducing themselves on tape using the wrong names. For example, Ricky said, "This is Darby" while talking in a funny voice, then Darby disguised her voice and introduced herself as Rachel.

WHY DID THE MOOSE CROSS THE ROAD?

When everyone has arrived, turn off the CD. Have kids put away their student page and circle up with their crews, sitting knee-to-knee so conversation will be easier. Help any newcomers find crews. Give kids a chance to shake hands and introduce themselves to anyone new in the crews.

SAY: Last week we each chose a Daily Challenge to complete to show our friendship with Jesus. Let's take a minute or two now to see how that went!

Choose two or three kids or leaders to tell which Daily Challenge they picked and what happened when they carried it out. Then have everyone share in his or her crew so each Daily Challenge is heard.

SAY: We want to celebrate the growth of our friendship with Jesus and with others, so each week we're adding links to a Friendship Chain.

Point out the progress made on the Friendship Chain last week, then have each child who completed a Daily Challenge add one link to the chain. If you have several crews, help them work together as they attach their last links so the chains for each crew are joined into one chain. Then add this to the big Friendship Chain. Have leaders put aside the supplies and hold up the chain.

SAY: Look at how you're spreading the love and friendship of Jesus! Now let's play a fun game to help us get to know more about each other.

SUPPLIES & MATERIALS

You'll need bright-colored construction paper, tape, and scissors.

MOOSE TRACKS

Is your Friendship Chain getting long? Find a way to celebrate with your entire church. Let kids parade through an adult gathering holding their chain, or hang it in the hallway one week with a poster explaining how the chain grows each week. Let people know that kids are making a difference as they grow in their friendships with Jesus and others!

Calling kids by their names helps them feel special—learn names and use them!

SUPPLIES & MATERIALS

You'll need clean, soft blindfolds; the *Moose Mountain: Children's CD;* and a CD player.

MOOSE TRACKS

Make sure blindfolded kids know that they can touch anyone, not just people from their own crews.

Kids without blindfolds need to call out the "Wow!" response to all blindfolded players, not just those in their own crew.

GRINS & GAMES

Choose one child or leader from each crew to be blindfolded. Those with blindfolds can walk around the room normally. Others must walk on their knees or crawl.

Explain that in this game, the people who are blindfolded call out "Friends!" as often as necessary, and everyone else responds with "Wow!" The blindfolded children will listen to the responses and each try to reach out and touch someone. Whoever is touched changes places with the blindfolded player.

Let kids play for a few minutes until everyone is familiar with the game, then add to the challenge by playing tracks 1 and 2 on the *Moose Mountain: Children's CD.* This will turn the game into an even noisier activity, but it makes it all the more fun! Play until several children have had turns being blindfolded.

Turn off the music, gather the blindfolds, and have everyone return to their crews. As you ask the following questions, have children share their thoughts with their crews so everyone gets a chance to talk. **ASK:**

- **What made this game a challenge?**
- **Why was listening important in this game?**
- **If you were blindfolded, what could you tell from the voices you heard?**
- **Why is listening important?**
- **What can happen if we don't listen at school? at home? to our friends?**

SAY: This game helped us realize that listening can be important. Friends take time to listen to each other. Let's find out about a time Jesus listened and see what happened.

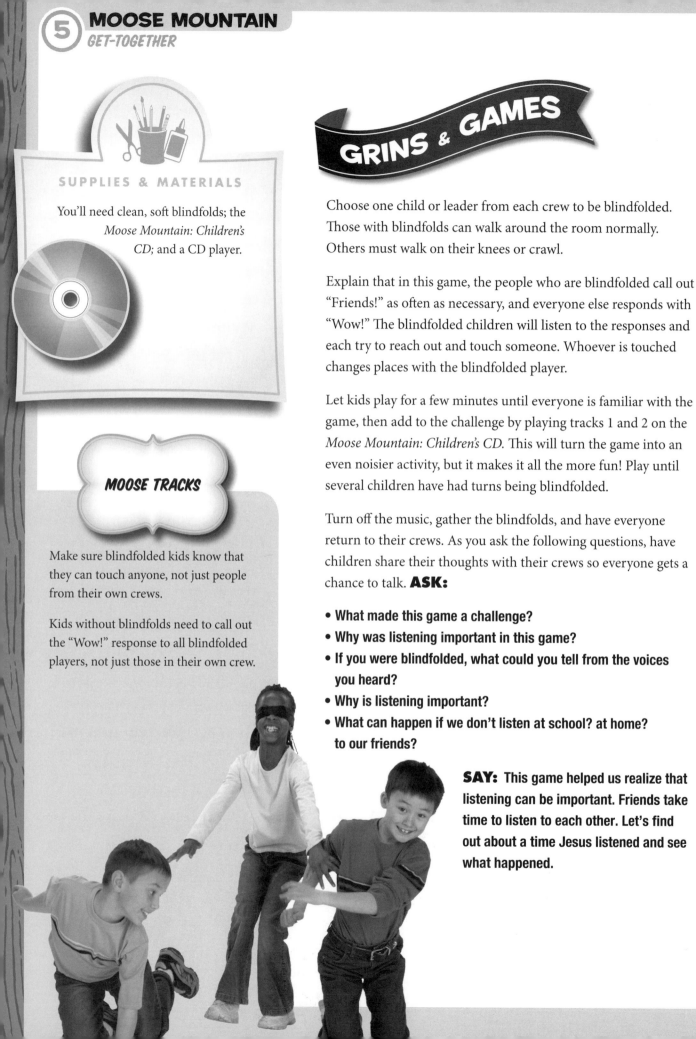

Getting to Know
JESUS

ALLERGY ALERT

See page 12.

SUPPLIES & MATERIALS

You'll need round crackers, cheese spread, paper plates, wet wipes, plastic knives, an assortment of chopped vegetables and grated cheese, and a Bible.

SAY: Our Bible story today is about some people who were cranky and some people who were happy. Let's make a snack that we can use to tell our Bible story. Each of you should make three or four cracker faces. Be sure at least one is happy and one is cranky.

Have children clean their hands with wet wipes or at a nearby sink. Then demonstrate how to spread a little cheese spread on a cracker and use the vegetables and cheese toppings to make a face on it. For example, sliced olives or small carrot chunks could be eyes, a sliver of red pepper could be a mouth, and a few bits of grated cheese could be the hair. Let kids have fun making happy and cranky faces for several minutes. Then have them put the faces they've made on their plates and return to their crews.

SAY: We're going to use our cracker faces to tell the Bible story. It comes from Mark 10:13-16. Show kids your open Bible. One day some parents took their kids to see Jesus. The parents wanted Jesus to touch their kids and bless them. In your crew, find some happy-face crackers that could be Jesus, the parents, and the kids. Give kids a minute to do this.

MOOSE TRACKS

Set up several areas for making snacks so kids can all work at the same time.

GO ALL OUT!

Go wild with the toppings you make available to kids. Grated cheese, grated carrots, and finely chopped olives make great hair, and red peppers and tiny chunks of tomato are fun for mouths. Raisins, sliced olives, sliced carrots, and celery bits make wacky eyes and noses. Explore the produce aisle and find the most colorful items!

FIELD TEST FINDINGS

Kids had fun squirting the cheese spread, and grated cheese was by far the favorite topping. Carrot slices and chunks turned out to be a popular topping since kids could cut or nibble these into different shapes.

MOOSE TRACKS

If you enjoy leading children in singing, try "Must Be Done in Love" (track 6) on the *Moose Mountain: Children's CD.* Lyrics can be found on page 174.

Getting to Know Jesus Continued...

Jesus was with his disciples and another group of men called Pharisees. The Pharisees thought they were pretty important, and they probably weren't the kind of guys who liked to hang out with children. The disciples were so concerned about taking care of Jesus that they weren't interested in a bunch of children, either. Sounds cranky to me. Find some cranky-face crackers to be the disciples and the Pharisees. Give kids a minute to do this.

The disciples told the parents and kids that they should go away and not bother Jesus. Which crackers show what you think the disciples' faces looked like? Which crackers show what you think the parents' and kids' faces looked like?

Jesus saw what was happening, and he was *not* happy! Find a cracker that's not happy. Let kids do this. Jesus told everyone, "Let the children come to me. Don't stop them!" Then Jesus took the children into his arms and blessed them. Find crackers that show what you think Jesus' face and the faces of the children and parents looked like then! Let kids do this. Find crackers that show how you feel when others listen to you. Let kids do this.

Now you can eat your crackers, and as you eat, you'll have a chance to talk about this Bible event with your crews.

As kids talk, have crew leaders help them discuss these questions:

• What would you have felt like if you were one of the kids whom Jesus welcomed?
• What do you think Jesus and the children talked about?
• What did Jesus show the grown-ups with his actions?
• How do you feel when someone takes time to listen to you?

SAY: 📖 Jesus listens to us. He lets us know that we're important to him by taking time to listen to us. When we pray, we're talking to Jesus. And when we pray, Jesus listens. Good friends listen to each other. Let's try that out!

TRY IT OUT!

SAY:  Ephesians 4:29 says, "Let everything you say be good and helpful, so that your words will be an encouragement to those who hear them." **ASK:**

- Do you think the words that others hear coming from your mouth are good and helpful?
- Are your words encouraging?
- Since ✝ Jesus listens to us, what kinds of words do you think he wants to hear?

Have kids remain in their crews, and make sure they're sitting in circles. Give each person a sheet of paper and a pen or pencil.

SAY: You are each going to write something nice about the person sitting to your left. Help children identify who they'll be writing about. **Without letting anyone see, write one nice word about that person on your piece of paper. If the person is kind, you could write "kind." If the person is funny, you could write "funny." Think of one thing you like about the person, and write that on the paper. Remember, don't let anyone see!**

Allow a minute for kids to each write a word on their paper. If you have mostly younger children, encourage the crew leaders to assist them. When kids have finished writing their words, have crew leaders help each child tape the word onto the back of the child it describes.

SUPPLIES & MATERIALS

You'll need paper, pens or pencils, and tape.

MOOSE TRACKS

If your students bring their Bibles to class or if you have a classroom set of Bibles, let kids look up verses as often as possible. It helps them become familiar with reading God's Word—and helps kids realize that the Bible is for them, not just for grown-ups!

FIELD TEST FINDINGS

Be sure to let kids know that others will eventually see what they're writing. In our field test, a secret crush was revealed when one boy wrote that the girl to his left was pretty. When others read this, both children were embarrassed.

FIELD TEST FINDINGS

Children loved being affirmed in this way! They were so pleased that others had kind thoughts about them.

Try It Out! Continued...

When everyone has done this (including leaders!), **SAY:** Now **I want you to give people clues about the words you can see on their backs. For example, if you see the word *kind* on someone's back, you can say, "You're someone who helps others," or "You are caring." Without actually saying the word, describe it. Then you can guess what's on your back. Move around so you can give clues and get clues from several people. You'll have to listen carefully to learn what others like about you.**

Let children move around and give clues for several minutes. Encourage leaders to get involved, too. Leaders with younger children in their groups will need to help them by whispering clues. When most children have figured out their words of affirmation, let them remove the paper from their backs. Those who did not figure out the clues can read their words. Have kids return to their crews. **ASK:**

- **Why was listening important in this activity?**
- **How did it feel to listen to people saying nice things about you?**
- **How does it feel when people don't use kind words?**
- 🕊 **Ephesians 4:29 says, "Let everything you say be good and helpful, so that your words will be an encouragement to those who hear them." How could you practice that this week?**

SAY: You have practiced several things that good friends do. You said nice things about each other. Friends do that. You encouraged each other. Friends do that. You listened to each other. Friends do that. ✝ Jesus listens to us, and he's a good example for us to follow. Let's get our Daily Challenges ready so we can practice listening this week.

See You Soon

Have each child cut out the Daily Challenge section of his or her student page. Read aloud the Daily Challenge options for this week, then have kids each choose and mark one option they're willing to commit to doing before your next get-together. When each child has chosen an option, show kids how to wrap their Daily Challenges around their wrists and secure them with tape.

SAY: I'm so thankful that 📖 Jesus listens to us. It helps me to have such a great example to follow. Now let's take time to talk to God about what's happening in the lives of our friends. We know he'll be listening!

Have the children share prayer needs in their crews and pray for one another. Then close the time in prayer.

Pray for the kids who are there, thanking God for listening to them and for desiring a relationship with each child. Ask God to help the kids as they listen to others and as they complete their Daily Challenges.

If time permits, play the "What's That?" track from the *Moose Mountain: Children's CD* (track 12) again so children who arrived late can have fun practicing listening. You can listen and offer your suggestions about each sound, too!

MORE TIME FOR FUN?

If you still have time, let kids work in their crews to complete the back side of their student page. Encourage kids to share their responses and thoughts with others in their crews. If kids don't have time to finish these reflections on the get-together, encourage them to take time at home this week to do so.

SUPPLIES & MATERIALS

Kids will need scissors, the Daily Challenge part of this week's student page, and pens or pencils. You'll also need a roll of tape.

THE *Daily* CHALLENGE

MOOSE TRACKS

If you have younger children or nonreaders, take time to read the Daily Challenges out loud and help them choose one for the coming week. The ideas have pictures beside them to help even nonreaders understand their choices.

You can have each child complete this sentence prayer: "Jesus, help me listen more to _____."

MOOSE MOUNTAIN

GET-TOGETHER

6

Bible Point: **JESUS LOVES US NO MATTER WHAT.**

Key Verse: **PROVERBS 17:17A**

"A friend is always loyal."

JESUS REINSTATES PETER.

Matthew 26:69-75; John 21:15-19

In Matthew 26:35, we find Peter declaring his loyalty to Jesus even unto death. But as we look at today's first passage, Matthew 26:69-75, we see Peter denying that he even knows Jesus—three different times to three different people. And then he leaves and weeps about what he has done. It is apparent that Peter felt grief and despair because he denied the one who meant so much to him.

This is the context in which we move to the second part of today's passage, John 21:15-19. Jesus has been crucified and has risen from the dead. He has appeared to his disciples. But we aren't told if Jesus has spoken directly to Peter since Peter's denials. No doubt Peter is wondering if Jesus will ever accept him again.

Jesus' questioning of Peter in John 21 may at times have seemed more than Peter could take. However, Jesus was pointing out that if Peter still loved him, Jesus had work for Peter to do. And Jesus ended the conversation using the same words he had used three years earlier to call Peter: "Follow me" (Matthew 4:19). Jesus loves us no matter what!

Making It Personal

- Read 2 Peter 1:1-2.
- What do these verses tell you about Peter's relationship with Jesus years later? How would you describe your relationship with Jesus?
- Pray: Lord, thank you for loving me even though I can be unlovable. Help me to be more loving when…

A Quick Overview

Activity	Kids will...	You'll need...
WOW!	Play and experiment with a variety of toys.	*Moose Mountain: Children's CD*, CD player (other supplies will vary—see activity)
WHAT'S NEW?	Share how they completed their Daily Challenges, and add to the Friendship Chain.	Bright-colored construction paper, tape, scissors
GRINS & GAMES	Play a game that brings smiles and practices friend making.	2 magnets, paper, pens or pencils, bowl
Getting to Know JESUS	Participate in the Bible account of Peter's denial of Jesus and his reinstatement.	Bible, honey sticks, wet wipes
TRY IT OUT!	Listen to and share ways others have hurt them.	Plastic adhesive bandages, pens
See You Soon	Choose a Daily Challenge to put what they've learned into practice.	Items used in "Wow!" activity, Get-Together 6 page from *Moose Mountain: For Kids*, pens or pencils, tape, scissors

SUPPLIES & MATERIALS

You'll need the *Moose Mountain: Children's CD* and a CD player. Other supplies will vary depending on which activities you decide to do.

GO ALL OUT!

Bring in a gentle dog, and let the children pet or brush the animal. Talk about how dogs are considered loyal animals. What does that mean? Be sure to supervise children and the dog at all times, and be considerate of children with pet allergies.

WOW!

Before kids begin arriving, turn on the *Moose Mountain: Children's CD,* and play songs from tracks 1-10 as they arrive and play.

Set up a variety of play areas in your room. Choose at least two of the following ideas.

• Paddle ball games: Provide several paddles that have small balls attached with a stretchy band. Kids can practice hitting the ball and then hitting it again when it zooms back to them.

• Velcro paddles and balls: These paddles and balls have Velcro on them so kids can easily catch balls tossed their way. They are especially good for younger children since they're easy to use and it's hard to drop the ball.

• Magnets: Set out a variety of magnets, metal objects, and nonmetal objects. Let kids experiment with what sticks and what doesn't.

• Gooey stuff: Mix cornstarch and water into a paste. Place this in bowls, and let kids smush their hands into the paste and pick up pieces of it. The paste feels firm, but when someone tries to mold it, it loses its shape. Be sure to have wet wipes handy for cleanup.

As children arrive, let them explore the various areas you've set up and play and experiment with the supplies.

WHAT'S NEW?

When everyone has arrived, put the discovery items aside, and turn off the music. Have kids and leaders circle up with their crews, sitting knee-to-knee so conversation will be easier. Help any newcomers find crews. Give kids a chance to shake hands and introduce themselves to anyone new in the crews.

SAY: Last week we each chose a Daily Challenge to complete to show our friendship with Jesus. Let's take a minute or two now to see how that went!

Choose two or three kids or leaders to tell which Daily Challenge they picked and what happened when they carried it out. Then have everyone share in his or her crew so each Daily Challenge is heard.

SAY: We want to celebrate the growth of our friendship with Jesus and with others, so each week we're adding links to a Friendship Chain.

Point out the progress made on the Friendship Chain last week, then have each child who completed a Daily Challenge add one link to the chain. If you have several crews, help them work together as they attach their last links so the chains for each crew are joined into one chain. Then add this to the big Friendship Chain. Have leaders put aside the supplies and hold up the chain.

SAY: The love and friendship of Jesus is really growing around here! Now let's play a fun game to help us get to know each other better.

SUPPLIES & MATERIALS

You'll need bright-colored construction paper, tape, and scissors.

MOOSE TRACKS

Just a reminder that the strips can be cut quickly with a paper cutter. This will save you time if you have a large group.

FIELD TEST FINDINGS

As kids were sharing and working on their chains, they got an idea. "Can we do more loops if we do more Daily Challenges?" they asked. We let the whole group vote on it, and it was unanimous. From that point on, we let the kids add one loop for each Daily Challenge they completed, with four being the most they could add. Otherwise, we'd spend the whole get-together making chains!

You'll need two magnets, paper, pens or pencils, and a bowl.

MOOSE TRACKS

It's no fun when you can't see the action! Give each crew its own set of magnets so kids can experiment with the north and south ends themselves. Or place your magnets on an overhead projector so kids can see a magnified version of how the magnets attract or repel.

If you have mostly younger children or kids who can't write yet, have crew leaders take suggestions from the kids and write them on slips of paper.

GRINS & GAMES

Hold up the two magnets. **ASK:**

• **What happens when you put two magnets together?**

Explain that each magnet has a "north" end and a "south" end. When the north end of one magnet and the south end of another magnet are near each other, the magnets draw together quickly. But when two north ends or two south ends are put together, the magnets repel, or push away from each other.

SAY: Let's play a game where we pretend to be magnets. What I need you to do first is write down one thing that draws you closer to a friend, just like the north and south ends of a magnet, and one thing that pushes you away from a friend, just like the magnets with the same ends together.

Give each person two slips of paper and a pen or pencil. If kids need a little help, suggest things that might draw them to a friend, such as laughter, kind words, playing a sport together, or being in the same class. Then suggest things that might push friends apart, such as telling lies, gossip, or not sharing. Encourage kids to think of realistic situations that happen in their own lives. Then gather the papers in a bowl.

Have all the kids stand. **SAY:** When I read each idea you've written down, you'll quickly decide if this is an "attract" action or a "repel" action. If what I read attracts friends, pretend you're all magnets drawn together in a big clump. If what I read repels or pushes away friends, pretend you're magnets that are pushing away from each other.

Draw slips from the bowl, and read them aloud. If kids have included identifying information ("when Jenny hits me"), make it more general ("when someone hits me"). Read as many slips as you have time for, allowing time in between each one for kids to either clump together or run away from each other. Then have kids gather with their crews and discuss these questions:

- **What helps friends stay together for a long time?**
- **What actions or situations make it hard to stay friends with someone?**

SAY: Most friendships go through hard times where the friends aren't sure if they should stick together or not. ✝ Jesus loves us no matter what and helps us find ways to stick with our friends—even when they aren't perfect. Let's check out what happened to Jesus and see what kind of friend he is.

FIELD TEST FINDINGS

Kids quickly got the idea of this game and had a lot of fun. What impressed us were the honest examples they gave of things kids really do that attract or repel. Some of the "repel" ideas were kicking others, calling names, or not inviting someone to a birthday party. "Attract" ideas included opening doors for others, calling someone on the phone to talk, and sharing.

MOOSE TRACKS

If you have a larger meeting room, you might post the discussion questions on an overhead projector or on a PowerPoint system. This allows each group to remember the questions and move ahead in discussion at its own pace. Or provide each crew leader with his or her own *Moose Mountain: Children's Leader Guide*.

SUPPLIES & MATERIALS

You'll need a Bible, honey sticks, and wet wipes.

MOOSE TRACKS

Honey sticks are plastic straws filled with honey that often come in a variety of flavors. If your grocery store doesn't carry these, try a health food or natural foods store. Kids can bite open the end, or you can snip them open with scissors. The honey is still sticky, but it's a lot less messy inside the tiny tubes.

FIELD TEST FINDINGS

The kids in our test group loved the honey! And by serving it in these handy straws, there was no mess.

Getting to Know JESUS

ALLERGY ALERT
See page 12.

SAY: We're learning that ✝ Jesus loves us no matter what. Another way to say this is that Jesus sticks with us. So while we learn about Jesus sticking with a friend, let's have a sticky snack.

Have children clean their hands with wet wipes or at a nearby sink, then distribute honey sticks for children to enjoy while you begin the Bible story.

Hold up your Bible and **SAY: The Bible tells us about one of Jesus' best friends, a man named Peter. I need someone to be Peter in our Bible drama. I need someone who will be loud and bold!** Choose a volunteer to be Peter, and have the person stand in the front of the room.

Peter was a fisherman. Peter, show us the muscles you've gotten from pulling in nets filled with fish. Encourage "Peter" to flex his muscles. **Peter was one of Jesus' best friends. In fact, one night when Jesus and his friends were having dinner, Peter told Jesus, "Even if everyone else deserts you, I never will." Peter, let's hear**

MAY I PLEASE HAVE A CINNAMON-FLAVORED HONEY STICK?

I WANT A PINK ONE... PRETTY PLEASE.

you say, "I never will!" as if you're the truest friend in the world! Have Peter say this line with enthusiasm. **Jesus answered Peter, saying, "Peter, the truth is that this very night, before the rooster crows, you will deny me three times." Jesus was saying that before the next morning, Peter would tell people he didn't even *know* Jesus! Peter, what do you have to say for yourself?** Let Peter respond, then **SAY:** **The Bible tells us that Peter actually said, "No! Even if I have to die with you, I will never deny you!" Who would like to have a friend like Peter?** Let kids respond and share why they'd want a friend like Peter. **I'd want a friend this loyal! Let's see what happened next.**

Later that night, soldiers came and arrested Jesus. They didn't like Jesus saying that he was God, so they decided to kill him! All of Jesus' friends got scared—they didn't want to be killed, too, so most of them ran away to hide. Peter decided to watch from a distance. He waited outside the place Jesus was being held. Peter, have a seat while you wait. Let Peter sit down. **While Peter was sitting in the courtyard, a servant girl came over and said to him, "You were one of those with Jesus." Hmmm…do you think Peter is going to say, "Yes, I was" or "No, I wasn't"?** Let kids clap or raise their hands to show their opinion. **The Bible says that Peter said, "I don't know what you're talking about." Peter, can you say that for us?** Let Peter repeat this line.

A little later, another servant girl saw him and said to some others, "This man was with Jesus." What's Peter going to do? Let kids call out their opinions. **Peter said, "I don't even know the man." Peter, can you say that for us?** Let Peter repeat this line with feeling.

And then even later, some other people said they thought Peter was one of Jesus' followers. What do you think Peter did? Let kids respond. **You're right! He said, "I don't know the man."** Let Peter repeat this line. **Immediately, a rooster crowed.** Have all the kids crow like roosters. **Peter remembered what Jesus had said, and he began to cry. ASK:**

• **Do you think Peter was a good friend? Why or why not?**
• **How do you think Jesus treated Peter after that?**

SAY: **Well, let's find out. The soldiers did kill Jesus, and they buried him in a grave. But three days later, Jesus rose from the**

Getting to Know Jesus Continued...

dead! And he eventually got a chance to talk to Peter.
If you were Jesus, what would you say to Peter?

We'll need someone to be Jesus to finish the drama. Have a
volunteer stand beside Peter. **Jesus said to Peter, "Do you love
me?"** Let "Jesus" repeat this line. **And Peter responded, "Yes,
Lord, you know I love you."** Let Peter say this. **Jesus said, "Then
feed my lambs." What do you think Jesus meant by that?** Let
kids share their thoughts, then **SAY: Jesus was giving Peter
responsibility for leading his followers. Then Jesus and Peter
repeated this same conversation again.** Point to Jesus and Peter,
and have them say...

Jesus: Do you love me?
Peter: Yes, Lord, you know I love you.
Jesus: Then feed my lambs.

SAY: And then Jesus asked Peter *again*! Have your actors
repeat the same conversation once more. **Finally, Jesus said,
"Follow me."**

Thank your volunteers, then have children gather with their
crews for discussion. **ASK:**

• **What about Jesus' conversation with Peter surprised you?**
• **Do you think Peter deserved forgiveness? Why or why not?**
• **Do you think you could treat your friends as Jesus did? Why or
  why not?**
• **Have you ever been thankful for a friend who loved you when
  you weren't a good friend? What happened?**

**SAY: Loving your friends no matter what is one of the hardest
parts of being a friend. Friends do a lot of things that push us
away, like in our game that we played earlier. But** 💜 **Proverbs
17:17 says, "A friend is always loyal." What does that mean to
you?** Allow kids to share responses.

**This verse reminds us that we need to treat our friends the way
we want to be treated, and we need to understand that no friend
except Jesus is perfect. Friends sometimes hurt us, so we need to
be willing to forgive. Let's do an activity that helps us think about
this more.**

TRY IT OUT!

SUPPLIES & MATERIALS

You'll need one plastic adhesive bandage and pen per person.

Have crew leaders and children form pairs. If there is an uneven number of people, form one group of three. Give each person a plastic adhesive bandage (still in the paper wrapper) and a pen. Ask children to leave the bandages inside the wrappers.

SAY: We use bandages to cover cuts and other small injuries. Think about a cut or scar you've had, and tell your partner about it. Kids can share about things as significant as broken bones and surgeries or as small as skinned knees and scratched arms. Be sure each partner has a turn to share, then **SAY:** The injuries you just shared can usually be covered by a bandage. But there are other injuries that are inside of us, and they can hurt just as much as a cut. Tell your partner about a time someone hurt your feelings and what that was like.

Allow time for partners to talk, and again be sure that each person has an opportunity to share. Then **SAY:** We've learned from how Jesus treated Peter that ✝ Jesus loves us no matter what. We know from what we've told our partners that it can be hard to love someone who has hurt our feelings and not been a good friend to us. I'd like you to pray for your partner and ask God to help your partner forgive the person who hurt his or her feelings.

Have children pray in their pairs. Encourage them to pray aloud, but if children are uncomfortable with this, let them pray together silently. Then have children each write their name on the wrapper of their bandage and exchange it with their partner. **SAY:** Take your partner's bandage home, and put it in a place where you'll see it this week. Every time you see it, pray for your partner and the situation he or she shared with you. Friends help each other to be good friends.

MOOSE TRACKS

This activity can lead to difficult sharing. Encourage children to be caring and kind as they listen to their partners talk. Remind them that this is real-life practice and they're putting what they're learning into action. Talk to your crew leaders ahead of time so they're aware that some children may reveal deep hurts. If children tell of abuse, be ready to follow your church or state guidelines for handling these situations.

If your whole church is participating in Moose Mountain, let kids know that their older siblings and parents have also done this activity and are praying for people as well. Suggest that kids invite their family members to pray together for their "Band-Aid" partners this week.

SUPPLIES & MATERIALS

Kids will need scissors, the Get-Together 6 page from their *Moose Mountain: For Kids* books, and pens or pencils. You'll need the items used in the "Wow!" activity and a roll of tape.

CD-ROM

MOOSE TRACKS

If you enjoy leading kids in singing, try "What a Friend We Have in Jesus" (track 2) on the *Moose Mountain: Children's CD.* Lyrics are on page 172.

See You Soon

Have kids look at the "What Kind of Friend Am I?" section of their student page. Hold up the various items used in the "Wow!" section of today's get-together as kids find those same items on their pages. As you hold up each item, ask kids how these might represent either loving others no matter what or today's Bible story about Jesus and Peter. Older kids may want to write words or phrases on their student page that express how these items represent what they've learned today.

- For the paddle ball games, kids might suggest that the ball always returns to the paddle, just as true friends always return to each other. Or, since the paddle pushes the ball away, the paddle could be Peter pushing Jesus away, and the ball could be Jesus returning to Peter.

- The Velcro paddles and balls could represent friends who stick together, just as Jesus stuck with Peter even when Peter wasn't such a good friend.

- The magnets could represent actions that draw us to friends and actions that push us away. Kids might also notice that it's hard to push magnets away from each other since one will often spin around and attract to the other. This might represent the forgiveness Jesus showed to Peter.

- The gooey stuff holds its shape in certain situations but then gets runny and loses its shape when picked up. This is a more abstract concept, but older kids can make the connection that true friends don't change when the situation changes—they remain the same.

SAY: As you look at these items, think about what kind of friend you are and which of these items represents you best. Do you return to your friends even when they push you away? Do you stick with friends in tough situations? Do you forgive friends even when they hurt you? Are you a friend that stays true even when the situation is tough? Which of these objects describes

you as a friend? Let children silently reflect on these questions for a moment, then encourage kids to circle the object that shows which kind of friend they think they are—or kids might prefer to circle the item that shows the kind of friend they want to be. Ask children to take their papers home so they can be reminded of how to love others no matter what.

Have each child cut out the Daily Challenge section of his or her student page. Read aloud the Daily Challenge options for this week, then have kids each choose and mark one option they're willing to commit to doing before your next get-together. When each child has chosen an option, show kids how to wrap their Daily Challenges around their wrists and secure them with tape.

SAY: I'm so thankful that  Jesus loves us no matter what. It helps me to have such a great example to follow. Now let's take time to talk to God about what's happening in the lives of our friends. We know he'll be listening!

Have the children share prayer needs in their crews and pray for one another. Then close the time in prayer.

Pray for the kids who are there, thanking God for loving them no matter what and for desiring a relationship with each child. Ask God to help the kids as they demonstrate love to others and as they complete their Daily Challenges.

If you have younger children or nonreaders, take time to read the Daily Challenges out loud and help them choose one for the coming week. The ideas have pictures beside them to help even nonreaders understand their choices.

You may want to have each child complete this sentence prayer: "Lord, help me to stick with _____ no matter what."

MORE TIME FOR FUN?

If you still have time, let kids work in their crews to complete the back side of their student page. Encourage kids to share their responses and thoughts with others in their crews. If kids don't have time to finish these reflections on the get-together, encourage them to take time at home this week to do so.

GET-TOGETHER

7

Bible Point: **JESUS TRUSTS HIS FRIENDS.**

Key Verse: **PROVERBS 3:5a**
"Trust in the Lord with all your heart."

HOLY
BIBLE

JESUS SENDS OUT THE DISCIPLES IN PAIRS.

Mark 6:7-13

In today's passage, Jesus' disciples had been following him for some time. They'd been watching Jesus, soaking in his teachings, and learning from him. Now it was time for them to go out and put into action the things they'd learned. This step in Jesus' ministry made sense, as Jesus knew that one day he'd no longer be with his disciples on earth physically, and they'd need to be able to take action themselves. And Jesus certainly was able to reach more people with his message and influence by sending out the disciples.

Why did Jesus send out the disciples in pairs? It may have been to give their message strength: According to Jewish law, a second or third witness was needed to lend authority to one person's statement. And, of course, having a second person along on a difficult mission gave both people someone to turn to for encouragement when things got tough.

Upon reading Mark 6:8-9, one might question, "How were the disciples to survive?" They were to depend on God to provide for their needs. They lived in a culture where it was common for people to invite travelers into their homes for food and a place to sleep, but certainly setting out on a mission with so little must have taken a lot of faith.

It also must have taken a lot of faith on Jesus' part to trust these friends with his all-important message. But Jesus had lived with them and trained them, and he trusted them. And as we see in Mark 6:12-13, their mission was successful.

Making It Personal

- Read Ecclesiastes 4:9-12.
- How do these verses apply to your friendships? How is trust implied in this passage?
- Pray: Dear God, help me to be more trustworthy in the area of…

A Quick Overview

Activity	Kids will...	You'll need...
WOW!	Accept secret missions to complete during today's get-together.	Photocopies of "Your Mission" handout (p. 170), scissors, pen, envelopes, *Moose Mountain: Children's CD*, CD player
WHAT'S NEW?	Share how they completed their Daily Challenges, and add to the Friendship Chain.	Bright-colored construction paper, tape, scissors
GRINS & GAMES	Play a game that brings smiles and practices friend making.	*Moose Mountain: Children's CD*, CD player
Getting to Know JESUS	Write a secret mission for Jesus' disciples to follow.	Bibles, paper, pens or pencils, envelopes
TRY IT OUT!	Trust partners to carefully feed them a potentially messy snack.	Pudding cups, spoons, wet wipes, paper towels
See You Soon	Choose a Daily Challenge to put what they've learned into practice.	Get-Together 7 page from *Moose Mountain: For Kids*, pens or pencils, tape, scissors

I WONDER WHAT KIND OF PUDDING WE'RE HAVING. MAYBE IT WILL TASTE LIKE CHOCOLATE MOUSSE!

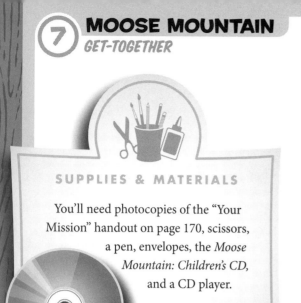

SUPPLIES & MATERIALS

You'll need photocopies of the "Your Mission" handout on page 170, scissors, a pen, envelopes, the *Moose Mountain: Children's CD*, and a CD player.

MOOSE TRACKS

If you have younger children who can't read yet, have their crew leaders whisper their missions to them.

Leaders can have secret missions, too!

GO ALL OUT!

Wear "authentic" spy attire (a trench coat, hat, and dark glasses for those of you who've never been spies!). Dim the lights, and provide flashlights so kids can have more fun as they sneak around.

WOW!

Before kids arrive, photocopy the "Your Mission" handout, and cut it apart as indicated. Place the sections in envelopes, and write things like "Secret Mission! For Your Eyes Only!" or "Spy Assignment!" on the envelopes. Set the envelopes on a table near the room's entrance, and turn on "Spy Music" (track 13) on the CD. Replay this track until you are ready to move to the next activity.

As kids arrive, whisper a greeting to them, **SAYING: You've been entrusted with a secret mission!** Let each person choose from the selection of envelopes. Tell kids to open their envelopes and read their missions but not to tell anyone else what their missions are. As kids begin their missions, ask them about the biggest or most important job anyone has ever trusted them to do.

Tell kids to try to complete their secret missions before the end of the get-together. They can start right then, or they can wait a little while so others won't be suspicious of what they're up to!

When everyone has arrived, turn off the music, and put the remaining secret-mission envelopes aside. Have kids and leaders circle up with their crews, sitting knee-to-knee so conversation will be easier. Help any newcomers find crews. Give kids a chance to shake hands and introduce themselves to anyone new in the crews.

SAY: Last week we each chose a Daily Challenge to complete to show our friendship with Jesus. Let's take a minute or two now to see how that went!

Choose two or three kids or leaders to tell which Daily Challenge they picked and what happened when they carried it out. Then have everyone share in his or her crew so each Daily Challenge is heard.

SAY: We want to celebrate the growth of our friendship with Jesus and with others, so each week we're adding links to a Friendship Chain.

Point out the progress made on the Friendship Chain last week, then have each child who completed a Daily Challenge add one link to the chain. If you have several crews, help them work together as they attach their last links so the chains for each crew are joined into one chain. Then add this to the big Friendship Chain. Have leaders put aside the supplies and hold up the chain.

SAY: The love and friendship of Jesus is really growing around here! Now let's play a fun game to help us get to know each other better.

SUPPLIES & MATERIALS

You'll need bright-colored construction paper, tape, and scissors.

MOOSE TRACKS

Is your chain really growing? Be sure to celebrate the kids' growth! Make a big deal of how wonderful it is to let our friendship with Jesus show!

FIELD TEST FINDINGS

By now our chain had really taken off. The kids had set a goal of having it reach across the room—and they'd already met the goal! They were really psyched about doing the Daily Challenges.

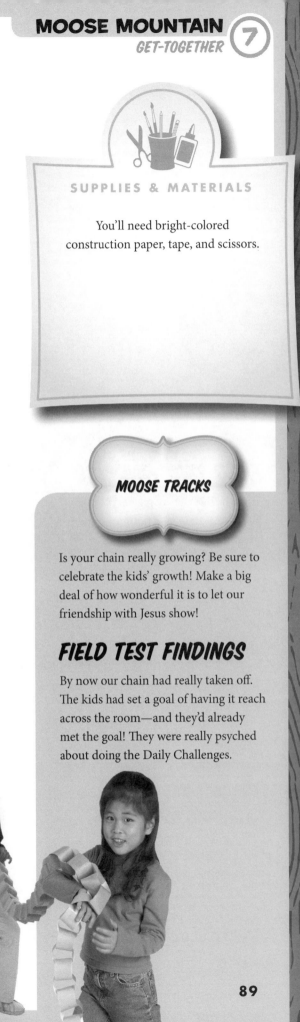

SUPPLIES & MATERIALS

You'll need the *Moose Mountain: Children's CD* and a CD player.

FIELD TEST FINDINGS

This game got lots of giggles! The kids had a great time with both roles and begged for more time to play.

GRINS & GAMES

Have kids and leaders form pairs. **SAY:** You received secret missions from me when you came in today, and you can work on completing those assignments throughout our get-together. But now I want you to give your partner a special mission to complete. The person in your pair who is the shortest will be the Sender. Have each pair identify who that person is. **Senders, your job is to send your partner around the room with specific missions of encouragement to complete. For example, you might say, "Go over to** [name of boy in room] **and say, 'I like your shirt.'" Or you might say, "Go over to** [name of girl in room] **and offer to tie her shoes for her." You've got a tough job because you have to think of things for your partner to do to encourage others in the room. Partners, you're the Doers. You have to do whatever your Sender tells you to do. You get to be the ones who encourage others! Everyone ready? Go!**

Play "With All Your Heart" (Proverbs 3:5-6) (track 4) on the *Moose Mountain: Children's CD* as Senders and Doers complete their missions. After a few minutes, have Senders and Doers switch roles. Continue the game for a few more minutes, then turn off the music and have kids gather with their crews for discussion. **ASK:**

• **Which job was easier? Why?**
• **Were you able to complete all the jobs your Sender gave you? Why or why not?**

SAY: It's fun to give people jobs, and it's fun to encourage others and do nice things for them. I'm glad you could all be trusted with these missions. Today we're learning that ✝ Jesus trusts his friends. Let's look in our Bibles to find out about the mission he gave his friends.

Provide each crew with a Bible, paper, a pen or pencil, and an envelope.

SAY: You all trusted each other with special missions, and each of you is also completing a secret mission during our get-together. In the Bible, Jesus gave his friends a mission. I'd like you to read about this mission with your crew and then make a "secret mission" assignment for Jesus' disciples.

Have crews read Mark 6:7-12 aloud together. If you have crews with younger children who can't read yet, ask the crew leaders to read the passage aloud. When the crews have finished reading, say: **Pretend that Jesus asked you to write down the mission he was sending his disciples on. Use your supplies to write down the secret mission Jesus gave his friends, and seal it inside your envelope.**

Allow time for crews to do this. When each crew has finished, have crews exchange envelopes. **SAY:** Open your envelope, and choose one person to read aloud what another crew has written. When crews have done this, **ASK:**

- If you were one of Jesus' disciples, how would you have felt when you heard about the job Jesus had for you?
- Do you think you would be able to do this job? Why or why not?
- Why do you think Jesus sent out his friends in pairs instead of by themselves?
- How does this mission show that  Jesus trusts his friends?
- Our verse today is 💧 Proverbs 3:5, which says, "Trust in the Lord with all your heart." How do you think this verse might have helped the disciples?
- How can this verse help you?

SAY: Jesus gave his friends a job that might have been scary for them. It was a big job! But Jesus trusted his friends to do this important task. And they had to trust God to help them do the job Jesus gave them. Jesus' example teaches us that *we* should trust our friends, too. Let's do an activity to help us practice trusting each other right now!

SUPPLIES & MATERIALS

You'll need Bibles, paper, pens or pencils, and envelopes.

MOOSE TRACKS

Crews of nonreaders can tell their leaders what to write for this activity.

Let kids know that they don't have to write down the mission word for word; they can give an overall idea of what the disciples were supposed to do.

If you enjoy leading kids in singing, try "With All Your Heart" (Proverbs 3:5-6) (track 4) on the *Moose Mountain: Children's CD*. Proverbs 3:5a is this week's verse, and this fun song is a great one for helping kids learn God's Word. Lyrics are on page 173.

If you only have one crew, you'll need to have the kids form two groups to complete this activity.

SUPPLIES & MATERIALS

You'll need pudding cups, spoons, wet wipes, and paper towels. You may want to provide cups of water, too.

FIELD TEST FINDINGS

This was hysterical! The kids were laughing the whole time they were doing this, but they managed to have only one accidental spill. Yes, a little pudding got on chins, but no one minded. The kids did like having a choice of pudding flavors. We provided both chocolate and vanilla.

TRY IT OUT!

ALLERGY ALERT
See page 12.

Have children clean their hands with wet wipes or at a nearby sink. Then have each person find a partner. **SAY:** **You're going to feed your partner a snack. This is a chance for you to show that you trust your partner, and it's a chance for you to show that you can be trusted. ASK:**

• **How would a friend feed his or her partner?**

Let kids respond, and affirm that friends would try not to spill the snack or get it on the partner's face or clothing.

Distribute the pudding cups and spoons. If you're brave, you can also distribute cups of water for partners to serve each other. Have paper towels and wet wipes handy for those who need them. Then have kids open the pudding cups and feed their partners, taking turns with bites of pudding. When kids have finished their snack and cleaned up, have them return to their crews for discussion. **ASK:**

• **Did your partner turn out to be trustworthy or not? Explain.**
• **What are some things you trust your friends to do?**
• **Are you a trustworthy friend? Why or why not?**
• **What can you do so your friends will be able to trust you more?**

SAY: **It's important to choose friends we can trust. Jesus didn't just give his special job to anyone—he trusted his closest friends with this job. We can choose friends whom we trust, and we need to be the kind of friend others can trust.**

See You Soon

Ask kids if they were able to complete the secret missions they were given at the beginning of today's get-together. See if kids can guess what other people's secret missions were.

SAY: It's fun to be trusted to serve others. I trust that each of you will complete your Daily Challenge this week, too!

Have each child cut out the Daily Challenge section of his or her student page. Read aloud the Daily Challenge options for this week, then have kids each choose and mark one option they're willing to commit to doing before your next get-together. When each child has chosen an option, show kids how to wrap their Daily Challenges around their wrists and secure them with tape.

SAY: I'm so thankful that ✝ Jesus trusts his friends. It helps me to have such a great example to follow. Our verse today, ❤ Proverbs 3:5, tells us, "Trust in the Lord with all your heart." One way we show that we trust God is by telling him what's going on in our lives. Let's do that!

Have the children share prayer needs in their crews and pray for one another. Then close the time in prayer.

Pray for the kids who are there, thanking God for trusting them and for desiring a relationship with each child. Ask God to help the kids as they demonstrate trust to others and as they complete their Daily Challenges.

SUPPLIES & MATERIALS

Kids will need scissors, the Daily Challenge part of this week's student page, and pens or pencils. You'll also need a roll of tape.

THE Daily CHALLENGE

MOOSE TRACKS

If you have younger children or nonreaders, take time to read the Daily Challenges out loud and help them choose one for the coming week. The ideas have pictures beside them to help even nonreaders understand their choices.

If you'd like, have each child complete this sentence prayer, filling in a situation from his or her own life: "Jesus, help me to trust you with _____."

FIELD TEST FINDINGS

Some kids were really secretive about their secret missions, and others did them quickly and obviously. Either way, kids got the message and had fun being trusted with a job.

See You Soon Continued...

Be sure that kids take home the top section of their student page. Tell kids that the front side has fun trust activities for them to try with their families and friends at home!

MORE TIME FOR FUN?

If you still have time, let kids work in their crews to complete the back side of their student page. Encourage kids to share their responses and thoughts with others in their crews. If kids don't have time to finish these reflections on the get-together, encourage them to take time at home this week to do so.

I'M SORRY I GOT PUDDING ALL OVER YOUR BEAK, ELLIE. CAN YOU STILL TRUST ME?

WELL, I GUESS SO, ESPECIALLY SINCE YOU DIDN'T LOSE YOUR TEMPER WHEN I DUMPED PUDDING ALL OVER YOUR SCARF.

MOOSE MOUNTAIN

GET-TOGETHER

8

Bible Point: **JESUS FORGIVES US.**

Key Verse: **JOHN 3:16**

"For God loved the world so much that he gave his one and only Son, so that everyone who believes in him will not perish but have eternal life."

HOLY BIBLE

JESUS DIES AND IS RESURRECTED.

Luke 23:32–24:12

At the request of the Jewish leaders, Pilate, the Roman governor of Judea, agreed to have Jesus crucified. It is significant that Jesus was crucified between two criminals. To the Jews, this indicated that he was a criminal. It seems likely that the religious leaders had exerted their influence to arrange for this positioning as one more way to humiliate Jesus.

When Jesus died, the skies became dark from noon until 3 p.m. There is no way to explain this darkness as a natural phenomenon. God must have darkened the sky. When this passage was written, hundreds of thousands who could attest to the accuracy of the statement would have still been alive.

The resurrection of Jesus is the most important event in human history. It proves that Jesus is the Son of God, and because of it we can be made right with God. If Christ had not been raised from the dead, the Christian faith would be a hopeless delusion.

More than once, Jesus had predicted his death and resurrection while he was with the disciples. They failed to believe him, misunderstood him, or forgot these predictions altogether. So on that first Easter morning, though it was the day on which Jesus had said he would rise from the dead, the women brought burial spices, expecting to find Jesus' dead body.

How somber their mood must have been as they approached the tomb. And how it must have made the discovery of an empty tomb and the encounter with two glorious angels all the more shocking! Jesus was, and is, alive!

Making It Personal

- Read Romans 6:4.
- How has your relationship with Jesus made your life brand new?
- Pray: Jesus, thank you for your forgiveness and for the new life I have through you. Help me to demonstrate my relationship with you to the children as I…

A Quick Overview

Activity	Kids will...	You'll need...
WOW!	Hammer nails.	2x4 lumber, nails, hammers
WHAT'S NEW?	Share how they completed their Daily Challenges, and add to the Friendship Chain.	Bright-colored construction paper, tape, scissors
GRINS & GAMES	Sing a song that brings smiles and practices friend making.	*Moose Mountain: Children's CD*, CD player, photocopies of page 173
Getting to Know JESUS	Have a variety of sensory experiences as they explore the events surrounding Jesus' death and resurrection.	Bible, items from "Wow!" activity, vinegar, cotton swabs, cups, red tempera paint, glitter, Get-Together 8 page from *Moose Mountain: For Kids*, wet wipes, doughnut holes
TRY IT OUT!	Put forgiveness into practice.	Mark-B-Gone pens, strips of white sheet, spray bottles, wooden cross from "Getting to Know Jesus" activity
See You Soon	Choose a Daily Challenge to put what they've learned into practice.	Daily Challenges from Get-Together 8 page, pens or pencils, tape, scissors

SUPPLIES & MATERIALS

You'll need two pieces of 2x4 lumber that are at least 3 feet long for every two crews, common nails, and hammers.

Before the session, place the lumber on the floor, and put the hammers and nails nearby. As children arrive, greet them by name, and direct them to the supplies. Let them pound nails into the wood. Remind kids to be careful with the hammers and to tap the nails gently to get them started in the wood. Have your leaders supervise this activity.

MOOSE TRACKS

Don't use finishing nails for this activity because the heads are too small for children to pound.

You may want to provide safety goggles for children to wear while they're hammering.

Provide two pieces of lumber for every two crews.

FIELD TEST FINDINGS

Kids *love* to hammer!

MAY I BORROW A HAMMER, ELLIE?

SURE, ROOFUS! JUST BE SURE YOU DON'T GET ANY SAWDUST ON MY FEATHERS— THEY'RE VERY DELICATE!

WHAT'S NEW?

When everyone has arrived, put aside the items from the "Wow!" activity. Have kids and leaders circle up with their crews, sitting knee-to-knee so conversation will be easier. Help any newcomers find crews. Give kids a chance to shake hands and introduce themselves to anyone new in the crews.

SAY: Last week we each chose a Daily Challenge to complete to show our friendship with Jesus. Let's take a minute or two now to see how that went!

Choose two or three kids or leaders to tell which Daily Challenge they picked and what happened when they carried it out. Then have everyone share in his or her crew so each Daily Challenge is heard.

SAY: We want to celebrate the growth of our friendship with Jesus and with others, so each week we're adding links to a Friendship Chain.

Point out the progress made on the Friendship Chain last week, then have each child who completed a Daily Challenge add one link to the chain. If you have several crews, help them work together as they attach their last links so the chains for each crew are joined into one chain. Then add this to the big Friendship Chain. Have leaders put aside the supplies and hold up the chain.

SAY: The love and friendship of Jesus is really growing around here! Now let's do a fun activity that will help us learn more about the kind of friend Jesus is.

SUPPLIES & MATERIALS

You'll need bright-colored construction paper, tape, and scissors.

SUPPLIES & MATERIALS

You'll need the *Moose Mountain: Children's CD*, a CD player, and photocopies of the song "We Will Live Forever" (John 3:16) on page 173.

MOOSE TRACKS

Most kids won't know what *perish* means. Explain that this word means "to die" and that when we have a friendship with Jesus, we will go to heaven to live forever.

GO ALL OUT!

Show a clip from the movie *Spirit* as an introduction to the Bible story. Fifteen minutes into the movie, the horse, Spirit, is captured by soldiers and forced to go to a fort where men try to "break" him. Relate the sadness of this scene to the sadness Jesus' followers must have felt as they watched him being crucified. Preview the clip first so you know where to start and stop the movie.

GRINS & GAMES

SAY: Our verse today is 👂 John 3:16. Some of you might already know this verse, but in case you don't, it says, "For God loved the world so much that he gave his one and only Son, so that everyone who believes in him will not perish but have eternal life." Let's listen to a fun song that can help us remember this verse.

Listen to "We Will Live Forever" (John 3:16) (track 5) once. Then hand out a few copies of the lyrics to each crew, and have kids work together to make up wild and active motions to the song. If you have several crews, you might divide the song among them, having one or two crews create motions for one section while a few other crews work on a different section. Even if crews are working on the same lyrics, they may come up with different motions. Allow a few minutes for kids to work together. It may help kids if you continue to softly play the song in the background.

When everyone is ready, play the song again, and let everyone sing and do the motions together. If you had crews work on different sections, let them teach the motions they created to the others.

Then **ASK:**

• What does this verse help us understand about Jesus?
• Why is the message of this verse so important?

SAY: This verse lets us know that God loves us so much that he was willing to let Jesus take the punishment for our sins. And if we believe in Jesus, we will be able to live forever in heaven with him someday. This is possible because ✝ Jesus forgives us. This is a really big deal! Let's find out more.

ALLERGY ALERT

See page 12.

SUPPLIES & MATERIALS

You'll need a Bible; two pieces of lumber, a hammer, and nails from the "Wow!" activity; vinegar; cotton swabs; cups; red tempera paint; glitter; wet wipes; and doughnut holes. Kids will need the "Remember Me" section of the Get-Together 8 page from their *Moose Mountain: For Kids* books.

CD-ROM

Before kids arrive, pour small amounts of vinegar into cups, preparing one cup for each crew. Prepare a small cup of red tempera paint for each crew as well.

SAY: Imagine that I did something wrong. Let's say I told a lie. Should I be punished for telling a lie? Let kids respond. **Yes, I should be punished. What would be a fair punishment?** Let kids offer suggestions. **Let's say that my punishment for telling a lie is no dessert for a week. I deserve that punishment. But what if** [name of child in group] **takes my punishment for me? Suppose** [name of child] **is willing to give up desserts so I can eat desserts, even though he** [or she] **didn't do anything wrong. Is that fair?** Let kids respond.

Hold up your Bible so children understand that what you're sharing comes from God's Word. **SAY: We know that all of us do wrong things. Those wrong things are called sin. When we sin, we deserve to be punished. The Bible says that the punishment for sin is death. But Jesus is willing to take our punishment! Jesus never did anything wrong, so it's not fair for him to take our punishment. The Bible tells us that Jesus was nailed to a cross. I'd like you to close your eyes and think about what this felt like for Jesus.**

As children quietly close their eyes, pick up two pieces of lumber, and place them in the shape of a cross. Pound in two nails where the pieces meet so the cross keeps its shape. As you pound, continue talking. **SAY: Soldiers drove nails into Jesus' hands and into his feet so he couldn't move. He was nailed to a cross made of wood.**

Tell kids to open their eyes, and lean the cross against a wall where children can see it.

SAY: Jesus let them do this because he loves each one of us. Let's thank Jesus for his love. If any children are comfortable praying aloud, let them do so. If not, go ahead and briefly thank Jesus for his love and his willingness to endure extreme pain for us.

MOOSE TRACKS

Set a quiet and somber tone for this activity. Encourage children to participate quietly and to think about what Jesus did for them as they participate in this experience.

FIELD TEST FINDINGS

We let kids know at this point that this get-together would feel different from the others. It would be quieter and more thoughtful. After this prompt, they settled down and were more reflective.

MOOSE TRACKS

For sanitary purposes, don't let children re-dip their cotton swabs.

Getting to Know Jesus Continued...

While Jesus was hanging on the cross, he became thirsty. The soldiers laughed at him. They put a sponge on a stick, dipped it in sour wine, and held it up to his lips. It must have been very bitter.

Give each crew a small cup of vinegar. Have each person quietly dip a cotton swab into the vinegar and touch this to his or her tongue to taste the bitterness. Let children know that even though the vinegar is bitter, it won't hurt them. **SAY:** **As you experience this bitter taste, think about someone who has made you feel bitter. Perhaps someone hurt your feelings or has been mean to you. Silently pray that God will help take away the bitterness you feel toward that person.** Allow a minute or two of silence while everyone does this. Then have children dispose of their cotton swabs.

Two criminals were hung on crosses beside Jesus. They were men who were being punished for what they'd done. One of the men laughed at Jesus and told him to prove he was God's Son by saving himself and both of them. The other man said, "We deserve to die for our crimes, but this man hasn't done anything wrong." Then he spoke to Jesus and said, "Jesus, remember me when you come into your Kingdom." Jesus answered, "I assure you, today you will be with me in paradise." Jesus was able to forgive this man and welcome him into heaven. I want Jesus to remember me, too! Let's write our names in red paint as a way of saying that we want Jesus to remember us, too.

Have children quietly dip their fingers in the red tempera paint and write their first names on the hillside pictured in the "Remember Me" section of their student page. Have kids place their wet pages in front of them on the floor. Provide wet wipes, and have leaders supervise children so they clean the paint from their fingers before moving on.

SAY: Finally, Jesus died. His friends were sad, and they took his body down from the cross and put it into a tomb, which is like a cave. Soldiers rolled a heavy stone in front of the opening, and everyone went home. **ASK:**

- How do you feel about what Jesus did?
- Why do you think Jesus was willing to take the punishment for your sins?

At this point, change your expression and tone of voice from one of sadness and somberness to one of amazement and joy. **SAY:** The amazing and wonderful thing is that Jesus didn't stay dead! Jesus has power over death, and after three days in the tomb, he came back to life! Jesus' friends went to the tomb on the morning of the third day and found the stone rolled away. Instead of Jesus' body, they saw two angels in dazzling robes who told them, "Why are you looking among the dead for someone who is alive? He isn't here! He has risen from the dead!" Because Jesus came back to life, our lives are changed!

Give each child a pinch of glitter to sprinkle over the wet paint on his or her student page to represent the amazing miracle of Jesus' resurrection and the change Jesus makes in our lives. **ASK:**

- **How do you think everyone felt now?** Allow time for children to share in their crews.

SAY: Jesus' friends must have been so excited! And we can be excited, too. Because Jesus had the power to come back to life, he has the power to forgive our sins. Let's have a fun snack to celebrate!

Have children clean their hands with wet wipes or at a nearby sink, then distribute the doughnut holes. Explain that these can represent the stone rolled in front of Jesus' tomb.

When children have finished their snack, have them clean their hands again and then gather with their crews for the next activity.

MOOSE TRACKS

For the best tie-in to the story, use glazed or plain doughnut holes. Avoid ones with coconut or sprinkles since these won't look much like stones.

If you enjoy leading kids in singing, try "Jesus, Jesus" (track 9) on the *Moose Mountain: Children's CD.* Lyrics are on page 175.

SUPPLIES & MATERIALS

You'll need Mark-B-Gone pens, strips of white sheet, spray bottles, and wooden cross you made in "Getting to Know Jesus" activity.

MOOSE TRACKS

Mark-B-Gone marking pens are water-soluble ink markers that are usually used for quilting and sewing. They're available at fabric and hobby stores.

If you have a large number of crews, you can set up more than one station for children to do this activity.

Encourage a reflective attitude during this activity.

Before children arrive, cut or tear an old white sheet into strips that are at least 4x12 inches. You'll need one for each person.

Give each person a strip of cloth. Provide each crew with at least one Mark-B-Gone marking pen. **SAY:** Jesus loves us so much that he was willing to take the punishment for our sins. Because of Jesus' death and resurrection, we can be forgiven. ✝ Jesus forgives us, and we can forgive others. Let's put that into practice right now.

Have each person think of someone he or she needs to forgive. Prompt kids to think of someone who has hurt their feelings, been mean, or broken a favorite toy. Then have each child use a Mark-B-Gone pen to write a word or phrase that represents this situation on a strip of cloth. Kids might write "mean words," "toy," or the initials (not the name) of the person they need to forgive. Children who don't write can draw a picture or make a symbol such as an X to represent this.

When each person has finished writing, say: ✝ **Jesus forgives us. It wasn't easy for Jesus to do this, and sometimes it's hard for us to forgive others, too. But friends forgive each other. I'd like you to silently pray and ask Jesus to help you forgive the person you wrote about on your cloth.**

After a moment of silent prayer, have children come up to the cross you made earlier, hang their strips of cloth over the crossbeam, and lightly spray the cloth with water from a spray bottle. The words on the cloth will disappear! Then have children return to their crews and circle up for discussion. **ASK:**

• Do you think it's hard for Jesus to forgive us? Why or why not?
• Is it hard to forgive others? Why or why not?
• Why is forgiveness important in a friendship?

SAY: Jesus loves us enough to forgive us. Let's get our Daily Challenges ready so we can keep practicing forgiveness this week.

Have each child cut out the Daily Challenge section of his or her student page. Read aloud the Daily Challenge options for this week, then have kids each choose and mark one option they're willing to commit to doing before your next get-together. When each child has chosen an option, show kids how to wrap their Daily Challenges around their wrists and secure them with tape.

SAY: I'm so thankful that ✝ Jesus forgives us. It helps me to have such a great example to follow. Now let's take time to talk to God about what's happening in the lives of our friends.

Have the children share prayer needs in their crews and pray for one another. Then close the time in prayer.

Pray for the kids who are there, thanking God for forgiving them and for desiring a relationship with each child. Ask God to help the kids as they demonstrate forgiveness to others and as they complete their Daily Challenges.

MORE TIME FOR FUN?

If you still have time, let kids work in their crews to complete the back side of their student page. Encourage kids to share their responses and thoughts with others in their crews. If kids don't have time to finish these reflections on the get-together, encourage them to take time at home this week to do so.

SUPPLIES & MATERIALS

Kids will need scissors, the Daily Challenge part of this week's student page, and pens or pencils. You'll also need a roll of tape.

MOOSE TRACKS

If you have younger children or nonreaders, take time to read the Daily Challenges out loud and help them choose one for the coming week. The ideas have pictures beside them to help even nonreaders understand their choices.

You can suggest that each child completes this sentence prayer: "Jesus, help me to forgive _____."

MOOSE MOUNTAIN

GET-TOGETHER

9

Bible Point: **JESUS SHOWS US HOW TO TREAT OTHERS.**

Key Verse: **PHILIPPIANS 2:3B**

"Be humble, thinking of others as better than yourselves."

JESUS WASHES HIS DISCIPLES' FEET.

John 13:1-17

It is especially significant that Jesus washed his disciples' feet because none of the disciples was willing to stoop below the others to do this demeaning task. The washing of feet, necessary because people in Jesus' day all wore sandals, was customary before the beginning of any meal and was normally done by a servant as guests entered the house. However, since this was a private meal, there apparently was no servant. The water, basin, and towel were there, and certainly the disciples thought about the fact that no one had washed their feet. But none of them took the initiative to do the washing before the meal. After the food had been set out, Jesus took action.

Peter's resistance of Jesus washing his feet showed that Peter didn't understand what was really happening, part of which was Jesus illustrating the cleansing power of his death. Peter also exhibited pride in his refusal to let Jesus wash his feet. He didn't yet understand that Jesus came to serve, not to be served.

Through his actions and words, Jesus commands us to serve one another as he served his disciples, although not necessarily in the washing of feet. To claim to be exempt from such service would be to claim to be greater than Jesus himself. And it would not be enough for the disciples to recognize that they were to serve one another; they needed to take action if they were to receive the blessing promised in John 13:17.

Making It Personal

- Read John 13:17.
- What is one thing you know Jesus wants you to do, but you are reluctant to do it?
- Pray: Lord, help me to be willing to serve you as you desire. Help me to model your actions to the children as I…

A Quick Overview

Activity	Kids will...	You'll need...
WOW!	Have the opportunity to wash their own feet.	*Moose Mountain: Children's CD*, CD player, water, towels, liquid hand soap, small wash basin
WHAT'S NEW?	Share how they completed their Daily Challenges, and add to the Friendship Chain.	Bright-colored construction paper, tape, scissors
GRINS & GAMES	Do an activity that brings smiles and practices friend making.	Get-Together 9 page from *Moose Mountain: For Kids*, scissors, *Moose Mountain: Children's CD*, CD player, variety of fabric as described in activity
Getting to Know JESUS	Observe a foot washing, and learn how Jesus treated his friends with kindness.	Bible, foot-washing supplies from "Wow!" activity
TRY IT OUT!	Put others first as they prepare, serve, and clean up a snack.	Wet wipes, sweet snack, sour snack
See You Soon	Choose a Daily Challenge to put what they've learned into practice.	Daily Challenges from Get-Together 9 page, pens or pencils, tape, scissors

SUPPLIES & MATERIALS

You'll need the *Moose Mountain: Children's CD,* CD player, water, towels, small wash basin, and liquid hand soap.

Before children arrive, begin playing tracks 9-10 on the *Moose Mountain: Children's CD.* Continue playing these tracks throughout this activity.

As children enter the room, welcome them by name. Invite them to remove their shoes and socks and wash their own feet before sitting down. Don't force anyone to participate, but gently encourage kids to get involved. Chat with kids about times they felt really grungy and dirty and couldn't wait to get clean.

MOOSE TRACKS

Tip off your leaders about this activity ahead of time, and ask them to participate by washing their feet as they enter. When adults and teens model this to the kids, they're more likely to participate themselves.

GO ALL OUT!

Provide the best! Make sure the water you supply is warm. Bring in fluffy towels, various scented lotions, several kinds of soap, and maybe even some foot powder.

CAN SOMEONE HELP ME WASH MY HOOVES?

I'VE GOT SOME BUBBLE BATH IN MY PURSE. I'LL USE THAT TO GET YOUR HOOVES SQUEAKY CLEAN!

When everyone has arrived, put the water and other supplies aside. Have kids and leaders circle up with their crews, sitting knee-to-knee so conversation will be easier. Help any newcomers find crews. Give kids a chance to shake hands and introduce themselves to anyone new in the crews.

SAY: Last week we each chose a Daily Challenge to complete to show our friendship with Jesus. Let's take a minute or two now to see how that went!

Choose two or three kids or leaders to tell which Daily Challenge they picked and what happened when they carried it out. Then have everyone share in his or her crew so each Daily Challenge is heard.

SAY: We want to celebrate the growth of our friendship with Jesus and with others, so each week we're adding links to a Friendship Chain.

Point out the progress made on the Friendship Chain last week, then have each child who completed a Daily Challenge add one link to the chain. If you have several crews, help them work together as they attach their last links so the chains for each crew are joined into one chain. Then add this to the big Friendship Chain. Have leaders put aside the supplies and hold up the chain.

SAY: The love and friendship of Jesus is really growing around here! Now let's play a fun game to help us get to know each other better.

SUPPLIES & MATERIALS

You'll need bright-colored construction paper, tape, and scissors.

FIELD TEST FINDINGS

By now, the chain from our field test was wrapping around the ceiling of our room. The kids were delighted to share with visitors the meaning of the loops and what they were doing to add to the length of the chain.

SUPPLIES & MATERIALS

Kids will need scissors and the "Handle With Care!" section of the Get-Together 9 page from their *Moose Mountain: For Kids* books. You'll also need the *Moose Mountain: Children's CD,* a CD player, and a variety of fabric as described in the activity.

CD-ROM

MOOSE TRACKS

Put out the word to your church members that you're looking for fabric scraps. People often have leftover fabric pieces they'll give or loan you.

If you have more than three crews, gather extra fabric samples, or cut the ones you have into smaller pieces so you can pass them around more quickly.

FIELD TEST FINDINGS

It was interesting to see that some children interpreted expressions differently than others. For example, some saw an expression as angry, while others saw it as sad. This allowed them to place their pictures on a variety of fabric samples.

Before your get-together, gather several different kinds of fabric. Look for fabrics with interesting and different textures, such as fleece or other soft and fuzzy fabrics, satin or other sleek and slippery fabrics, burlap or other coarse and rough fabrics, velvet or other plush fabrics, lace, and so on. You can also choose a variety of colors and designs. The more pieces you can gather, the better!

If you don't have fabric around your house or church and don't want to purchase any, look for items around your home that could be used instead. Consider a scratchy bit of sandpaper, a fuzzy blanket, a satiny robe, soft socks, and so on.

Provide scissors, and have children cut apart the pictures in the "Handle With Care!" section of their student page. Then have everyone sit in a large circle.

SAY: We're going to play a matching game that's different from any other kind of matching game. I'm going to pass around several different pieces of cloth. Each one has a different look and feel. Pass around the fabric samples, and let kids touch them. After each piece of fabric makes its way around the circle, spread it on the floor in the center of your circle.

Now look at the pictures you cut out. Match the expression on the face in each picture to a piece of fabric, and set the picture on the piece of fabric you think "matches" that expression. There's no right or wrong answer in this game, but you should be able to explain why you matched the picture with the fabric.

Play "Jesus, Jesus" (track 9) on the *Moose Mountain: Children's CD* as kids move around the room touching the fabric pieces and placing pictures on them. When it appears that most kids have finished, have everyone return to their crews, and turn off the music.

Walk around the room, and stop at various pieces of fabric. Comment on ones that have a lot of the same pictures on them. For example, a piece of pink satin might have a number of pictures of the smiling girl on it. Ask kids to tell why so many chose the same fabric for that picture. Another piece of fabric might have a wide variety of faces on it. Ask kids to tell why they placed these faces with this fabric. You don't have to stop at every piece of fabric, but comment on a variety so a number of children have an opportunity to share. Then have children discuss with their crews:

- Was it easy or hard to match faces with fabric? Why?
- Why do you think some people have "rough" personalities and some people have "smooth" or "soft" ones?

SAY: Some people tend to be kind, others can be more fun, other people might be silly, and others can be cranky. We often treat people with different personalities in different ways. For example, if you know someone tends to be cranky, you might treat that person with extra kindness. If you know someone who tends to be funny, you might act a little sillier around that person. How we treat people matters. Some people need extra care, but everyone needs to feel loved. ✝ Jesus shows us how to treat others. Let's check out something Jesus did that shows us how to treat others.

MOOSE TRACKS

You don't have to agree or disagree with kids' explanation of their choices. When possible, remain neutral with comments like, "Thank you for sharing," or "I've never thought of it that way."

Another way to illustrate different personalities is to hold up a rubber ball and a light bulb. Ask kids how each of these needs to be treated. A ball can be dropped and bounced. It's tough! A light bulb is more fragile and needs to be treated with care. Why are some people more fragile than others? How does this help us better understand how to treat others?

FIELD TEST FINDINGS

Early in this get-together, we learned that one of the adult leaders was suffering from a very bad headache. We challenged the kids to use their quietest voices during the whole gathering, and they went for it! It was an excellent, real-life example of treating others as Jesus would.

SUPPLIES & MATERIALS

You'll need a Bible and the foot-washing supplies from the "Wow!" activity.

Getting to Know
JESUS

ASK: **What are some disgusting jobs you hate to do or hope you'll never have to do?** Kids might respond with tasks such as cleaning toilets, changing diapers, shoveling out horse stalls, and so on.

Those are icky things that most of us would avoid! In Bible times, there were jobs that people didn't like to do as well. Everyone wore sandals back then, and the roads were made of dirt—not paved like we have today. They didn't have cars, so they walked everywhere. How do you think their feet felt at the end of the day? Let kids respond. **When we come in and get ready to eat, most of us are reminded by our parents to wash our hands before we eat. Well, in Jesus' time, servants would wash people's feet before they ate. That way everyone felt clean and refreshed instead of dusty and sweaty.**

The Bible tells about a time Jesus and his closest friends, his disciples, gathered for a special meal together. They were all ready to eat. The food was on the table. But there was a problem. No servant was there to wash their feet. What do you think these men should have done? Let kids share their responses. **Well, no one volunteered to do the dirty work. Jesus didn't say anything like, "Hey, Peter! Wash my feet!" or "John! Get up and take care of us!" Instead, the Bible says that Jesus got up from the table, took off his robe, wrapped a towel around his waist, and poured water into a basin. Then he started going around the room, washing the feet of his friends and wiping them dry with a towel. This is what Jesus did.**

Approach a child in your group, and ask the child for permission to wash his or her feet. If the child declines, simply move to another child. If you think the children in your group are unlikely to let you wash their feet, talk to one of your volunteers ahead of time. If two or three children turn you down, you can approach this person. But if possible, choose a child. Without a great deal of fanfare, remove the child's shoes and socks, then wash and dry the child's feet.

Have kids discuss in their crews:

- **What do you think Jesus' disciples thought of his actions?** Let kids share their responses.
- **Jesus' actions made a big impression on his friends. One of them, Peter, made a fuss about it. He was uncomfortable with Jesus treating him this way. Why do you think he was uncomfortable?**
- **Does it make you uncomfortable when people treat you with extra kindness? Why or why not?**
- **Is it easy or hard for you to treat others with extra kindness? Why?**
- **What about those dirty jobs? Is it easy or hard for you to do them for others? Explain.**

SAY: After Jesus washed his friends' feet, he told them, "I have given you an example to follow. Do as I have done to you." Jesus didn't mean that we have to go around washing each other's feet. He meant that we should treat others with kindness and be willing to serve them. Our verse, 💟 Philippians 2:3, explains it this way: "Be humble, thinking of others as better than yourselves." Let's try this out!

MOOSE TRACKS

If you enjoy leading kids in singing, try "We're a Circle of Friends" (track 3) on the *Moose Mountain: Children's CD*. Lyrics are on page 172.

FIELD TEST FINDINGS

The first child who was approached was willing to have her feet washed, and a few others were willing as well. Most of them thought it was more disgusting that our leader was willing to do this.

SUPPLIES & MATERIALS

You'll need wet wipes, a sweet snack such as cookies, and a sour snack such as sour candies or lemonade.

FIELD TEST FINDINGS

In our field test, we didn't choose a snack that was sour enough. Be sure you taste your snacks ahead of time. One suggestion is to use something like M&M's candies or Hershey's Kisses for the sweet snack and a more tart candy such as Skittles for the sour snack. Some candies tout their sourness on their labels—just be sure to taste these to make sure they're as sour as they claim to be!

Several children claimed that their mothers helped them feel sweet by giving them hugs after sour and terrible days. Way to go, moms!

TRY IT OUT!

ALLERGY ALERT
See page 12.

SAY: We're going to have our snack now. Let's think of ways we can practice treating others as Jesus would. What ideas do you have?

Let kids brainstorm ideas for thinking of others first during your snack time. Kids might suggest serving snacks to one another, helping to prepare the snack, cleaning up after the snack, and so on. Let them do as many of their ideas as possible. Include one they may not suggest: Have children form pairs and clean the hands of their partners with wet wipes as an act of service.

MOOSE TRACKS

Be sure to thank kids who volunteer to serve!

Then proceed with serving the snack using the children's ideas. Ask children to keep their snacks in front of them and not eat until you've given further directions.

When everyone has a snack, point out that one part of the snack is sweet, and the other part is sour. Have children eat the sweet item. **ASK:**

• **What are some sweet ways to treat others?**

Have kids eat the sour item. **ASK:**

• **What are some sour ways to treat others?**
• **Are you usually sweet or sour to friends? family members? teachers or coaches?**
• **When have you felt sour and the sweet actions of someone else made you feel sweet yourself?**

SAY: It's not always easy to think of others first, but Jesus gives us a great example to follow, and he'll help us treat others with respect and kindness. Let's get our Daily Challenges ready so we can start treating others as Jesus would right away!

See You Soon

Have each child cut out the Daily Challenge section of his or her student page. Read aloud the Daily Challenge options for this week, then have kids each choose and mark one option they're willing to commit to doing before your next get-together. When each child has chosen an option, show kids how to wrap their Daily Challenges around their wrists and secure them with tape.

SAY: I'm so thankful that ✝ Jesus shows us how to treat others. It helps me to have such a great example to follow. Now let's take time to talk to God about what's happening in the lives of our friends.

Have the children share prayer needs in their crews and pray for one another. Then close the time in prayer.

Pray for the kids who are there, thanking God for treating them with love and for desiring a relationship with each child. Ask God to help the kids as they treat others as Jesus would and as they complete their Daily Challenges.

SUPPLIES & MATERIALS

Kids will need scissors, the Daily Challenge part of this week's student page, and pens or pencils. You'll also need a roll of tape.

THE Daily CHALLENGE

MOOSE TRACKS

If you have younger children or nonreaders, take time to read the Daily Challenges out loud and help them choose one for the coming week. The ideas have pictures beside them to help even nonreaders understand their choices.

You might suggest that each child completes this sentence prayer: "Jesus, one person I need to treat more sweetly is _____. Help me to do this."

MOOSE MOUNTAIN

GET-TOGETHER

10

Bible Point: **JESUS CHALLENGES US.**

Key Verse: **1 TIMOTHY 4:12**

"Don't let anyone think less of you because you are young. Be an example to all believers in what you say, in the way you live, in your love, your faith, and your purity."

JESUS TALKS TO A RICH YOUNG MAN.

Matthew 19:16-30

The young man who came to Jesus was a walking success story. His financial investments had prospered, and he had acquired money and power. Now he was consulting Jesus to ensure his long-range prospects.

In the first few verses of this passage, it becomes apparent that the young man is not "getting" what Jesus is saying. Jesus says that only God is good. In verse 20, the young man responds to Jesus and claims to have kept all the commandments. That is not possible. No one has kept all the commandments perfectly. If that were possible, Jesus wouldn't have needed to die on the cross!

Jesus knew the young man's real problem. His possessions were too important to him. Jesus knew that the young man would put his many possessions ahead of any desire to be fully obedient to God. So Jesus confronted him with that problem by suggesting he do the one thing that would be hardest for him to do: sell his possessions and give them to the poor! When the young man was gone, Jesus spoke to his disciples about the need to give up a love of possessions in order to truly follow God.

Jesus' example of a camel going through the eye of a needle caught his disciples' attention. His disciples likely looked upon earthly riches as a sign of God's blessing. Jesus wanted them to see that possessions could be a barrier to truly following God.

Making It Personal

- Read Matthew 6:24.
- How does this verse challenge you?
- Pray: Lord, help me to put possessions in their proper place. Let me know if I'm too attached to my...

A Quick Overview

Activity	Kids will...	You'll need...
WOW!	Learn to juggle.	*Moose Mountain: Children's CD*, CD player, plastic grocery bags, scissors
WHAT'S NEW?	Share how they completed their Daily Challenges, and add to the Friendship Chain.	Bright-colored construction paper, tape, scissors
GRINS & GAMES	Try fun challenges that bring smiles and practice friend making.	Chairs, sliced bread, watch with a second hand, cups of water
Getting to Know JESUS	Re-enact the account of Jesus and the rich young man.	Bibles, napkins, popcorn, wet wipes, handful of play money, *Moose Mountain: Children's CD*, CD player
TRY IT OUT!	Practice confronting and challenging each other with mock scenarios.	Get-Together 10 page from *Moose Mountain: For Kids*, scissors
See You Soon	Choose a Daily Challenge to put what they've learned into practice.	Daily Challenges from Get-Together 10 page, pens or pencils, tape, scissors

I'M GOING TO FIND ELLIE AND SEE IF SHE'LL HELP ME WITH THESE CHALLENGES!

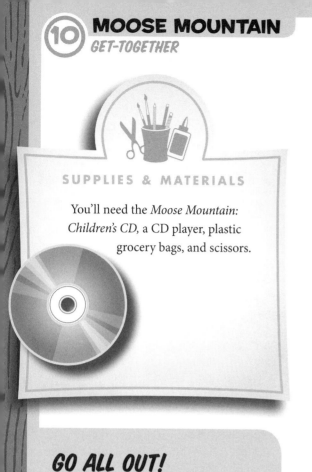

SUPPLIES & MATERIALS

You'll need the *Moose Mountain: Children's CD,* a CD player, plastic grocery bags, and scissors.

GO ALL OUT!

Invite a juggler to come put on a short show! See if someone in your church or community knows how to juggle, and ask this person to join your class for a demonstration and short lesson.

WOW!

Before children arrive, cut plastic grocery bags into two or three pieces each. Many jugglers learn the skill by using scarves, but these plastic pieces work just as well and are a *lot* less expensive!

Turn on the *Moose Mountain: Children's CD,* and play tracks 1-10 as children arrive. As children enter, welcome them by name and invite them to learn juggling skills. Some kids may already know how to juggle. If they do, they can help others (or you!).

Demonstrate how to begin practicing with one plastic "scarf." Hold the scarf in your right hand, then move your hand across your body and toss the scarf into the air near the left side of your head. Reach up with your left hand and catch the scarf. Repeat this several times until you're comfortable with this motion. Then it's time to move on to two scarves!

Hold one scarf in each hand. Toss the scarf in your right hand as before. As you let it go, toss the scarf in your left hand toward the right side of your head. With your left hand, catch the first scarf thrown, and with your right hand, catch the second scarf. Your arms will make a crisscross motion. Some jugglers use the phrase

"crisscross applesauce" to help them focus on this motion. Or you might suggest that kids remember to toss, toss, catch, catch.

Finally, add a third scarf. Hold two scarves in your right hand, and toss one of these first. Do the same motions you perfected with two scarves, but add in one more!

Keep the mood light. The plastic scarves float and are easy to catch, but a few kids may express frustration. Encourage them with words of affirmation and reminders that this is a skill that takes practice. As everyone practices juggling, ask kids about skills they've learned that are challenging. Riding a bike, learning to swim or dive, gymnastics, dance, hitting a softball, and using a computer are just a few examples of the many skills kids in your group may have.

SUPPLIES & MATERIALS

You'll need bright-colored construction paper, tape, and scissors.

When everyone has arrived, put aside the juggling items, and turn off the music. Have kids and leaders circle up with their crews, sitting knee-to-knee so conversation will be easier. Help any newcomers find crews. Give kids a chance to shake hands and introduce themselves to anyone new in the crews.

SAY: Last week we each chose a Daily Challenge to complete to show our friendship with Jesus. Let's take a minute or two now to see how that went!

Choose two or three kids or leaders to tell which Daily Challenge they picked and what happened when they carried it out. Then have everyone share in his or her crew so each Daily Challenge is heard.

SAY: We want to celebrate the growth of our friendship with Jesus and with others, so each week we're adding links to a Friendship Chain.

Point out the progress made on the Friendship Chain last week, then have each child who completed a Daily Challenge add one link to the chain. If you have several crews, help them work together as they attach their last links so the chains for each crew are joined into one chain. Then add this to the big Friendship Chain. Have leaders put aside the supplies and hold up the chain.

SAY: The love and friendship of Jesus is really growing around here! Now let's do a fun activity that will help us learn more about the kind of friend Jesus is.

ALLERGY ALERT
See page 12.

SUPPLIES & MATERIALS

You'll need chairs, sliced bread,
a watch with a second hand,
and cups of water.

SAY: Today we're learning that ✝ Jesus challenges us.
Some of you gave juggling a try as you came in today, and that's
certainly a challenge! Let's try a few more challenges to get us
thinking about the ways ✝ Jesus challenges us.

Lead children in the following challenges.

• Fast Jaw: Give each child a slice of bread. Explain that kids will
have exactly one minute to chew and swallow the bread. Give
the starting signal and let kids put their jaws in motion. This
challenge sounds easy, but it's not!

• Foot Lift: Have each child stand against a wall so the side of one
foot is flush with the wall (see illustration). The child's shoulder
should touch the wall. Don't let kids twist so their chests touch
the wall instead. Have each child put his or her other foot right
next to the foot that's touching the wall. Then ask kids to each
lift their outer foot.

MOOSE TRACKS

If you have a large number of crews, set
up three challenge stations that kids can
move between. Have a few of your crew
leaders assist you in leading these.

FIELD TEST FINDINGS

The kids in our field test were
determined to master these challenges.
They even found creative ways to…
um…well, to cheat. Be sure kids are
following your instructions in these
challenges. Challenge them to follow
directions!

← **WALL**

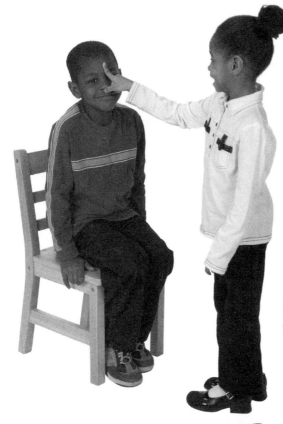

Grins & Games Continued...

• Muscle Finger: Have children form pairs. Have one child sit in a chair with his or her feet flat on the floor. Have the second child stand in front of the seated child and gently press one finger against the seated child's forehead. Then ask the seated child to stand up. Kids will be amazed at how strong they are using only one finger! Have kids switch places and try again.

When everyone has had a chance to complete the challenges, **SAY: Each of these challenges was impossible. But there's a way to meet each challenge. All it takes is a little help!**

Demonstrate how each challenge can be met. If kids have water to drink, they can eat the bread in one minute. Let a few kids who are still hungry and up for the challenge try this. For the Foot Lift challenge, demonstrate how having a friend, even one much smaller than you, offer you a hand allows you to lift your outer foot.

SAY: And if you're being held in your chair by someone with a strong finger, having a friend give you a little help will allow you to stand. Have a child come up and keep you seated in a chair with his or her finger. Then have a second child offer you his or her hands so you can get a bit of leverage to pull yourself out of the chair.

Friends can help us meet challenges, and friends can also challenge us to do what's right. ✝ Jesus challenges us. Let's find out how Jesus challenged a young man.

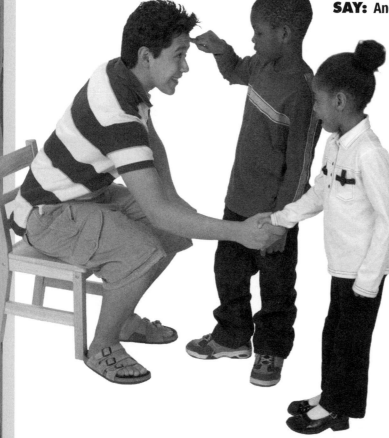

Getting to Know JESUS

ALLERGY ALERT
See page 12.

SUPPLIES & MATERIALS

You'll need Bibles, napkins, popcorn, wet wipes, a handful of play money, the *Moose Mountain: Children's CD*, and a CD player.

Have children clean their hands with wet wipes or at a nearby sink, then distribute napkins and popcorn for kids to snack on during your upcoming dramatic show.

Explain that the kids will see a drama based on a Bible account and that you need two volunteers. Everyone will listen to the story as it's told on the CD. The actors will follow along with the directions they hear and act out the scene for everyone. Choose one person to be Jesus and the other to be the rich young man. Give the child playing the rich young man the play money to hold and wave around.

Have "Jesus" stand on one side of your stage area and the "rich young man" stand on the other side. Play "Daily Challenge" (track 14) on the CD. When the drama is over, have everyone give your actors a round of applause, then have kids circle up with their crews for discussion. If kids want to refer to the Bible as they discuss, tell them they can find the account in Matthew 19:16-30. **ASK:**

- **What was the challenge that Jesus gave to the young man?**
- **Why didn't the man meet the challenge?**

SAY: Jesus challenged the man to do what was right. This can be really hard to do! When we see a friend doing something wrong—or not doing something right—we need to confront and challenge that person. For example, if you hear a friend calling his sister names, you need to challenge him to stop doing this and to show kindness to his sister instead. Share an example from your own life of how someone challenged you and how you responded. **ASK:**

- **Can you think of a time you had to challenge someone to do what's right? If so, what happened?**
- **When has someone challenged you to do what's right?**
- **Was Jesus mean or kind in his challenge? How can you tell?**

SAY: Because we are his friends and he cares about us, Jesus challenges us. Let's practice this!

Have kids put away any remaining popcorn and clean their hands again as necessary.

MOOSE TRACKS

No play money handy? You can cut a sheet of green construction paper into play bills. Make them a little more fun by drawing dollar signs on them.

FIELD TEST FINDINGS

Kids have so much fun being *in* the drama—not just watching. Our group of kids begged to participate each time we had a drama!

SUPPLIES & MATERIALS

Kids will need scissors and the "Can We Talk?" section of the Get-Together 10 page from their *Moose Mountain: For Kids* books.

CD-ROM

MOOSE TRACKS

The cards provide the situation, but they don't tell what the person should do. This gives kids an opportunity to consider what the right action is and then challenge their partners in this way.

If you have nonreaders, go over the cards together and explain each one. Kids will remember what they mean when they see the illustrations.

FIELD TEST FINDINGS

In our field test, the children wanted their partners to be clear that this was just pretend—they hadn't actually seen each other cheating on tests, and so on. With this disclaimer, they participated in a potentially difficult activity.

TRY IT OUT!

SAY: Our Bible verse is 🕊 1 Timothy 4:12. It says, "Don't let anyone think less of you because you are young. Be an example to all believers in what you say, in the way you live, in your love, your faith, and your purity." What do you think this means? Let kids respond. **This verse tells us that even if we're young, we can still be good examples for others to follow. People can tell that we're friends with Jesus by our actions. When our actions are *not* showing a friendship with Jesus, we might need a friend to challenge us.**

Have kids cut the "Can We Talk?" section of their student page into six sections as indicated. Have each child find a partner and sit down with the person. Choose a child to come up to the front as your partner so you can demonstrate what kids will do. Tell kids that they should pay attention to what you're doing.

SAY: You're going to mix up your cards and hold them facedown so your partner can't see what's on them. Then your partner will draw one of your cards and look at it. This card will tell your partner about a problem you're having. Then your partner will confront you and challenge you about this problem, and he or she will tell you what you should do to make the situation right. When your partner has finished, you'll do the same thing, drawing a card from your partner's stack.

Demonstrate this with your partner. Choose a card from your partner's stack, and read it aloud. Then challenge the partner to do what's right in a kind way. For example, if the card says, "I saw you cheating on a test," you might say, "I saw you cheating on a test in class today. I think you should admit to our teacher what you did." Then your partner can respond as he or she wants. Point out to the kids that sometimes a friend will accept our challenge and do the right thing. Other times, like the man Jesus challenged, they won't.

Let kids practice challenging their partners, then have them return the cards they drew. If time permits, have kids find new partners and repeat the activity. Then have everyone return to their crews and circle up for discussion. **ASK:**

- Was it hard or easy to challenge your partner? Why?
- Did you feel like your partner challenged you in a kind way? Why or why not?
- What makes it difficult to challenge friends?
- Why is it important to challenge our friends or be challenged by them?
- Do you think Jesus is challenging you about something in your life? If so, what?

SAY: Most of us have a lot of friends whom we wave to or just say "hi" to. But when we get to know someone better, our friendship becomes more special. One thing that makes a friendship strong is being able to say things that are hard and knowing that your friend will still love you. It's a risk because the friend might walk away, just as the man walked away from Jesus. But when friends stick together even in hard times, they know what true friendship is! Let's get our Daily Challenges ready so we can put this into practice this week!

MOOSE TRACKS

How are you as a leader? Is challenging others a challenge for you? One tip is to avoid accusations and attacks. Instead of saying, "You're a thief!" say, "I saw you looking through someone's purse. Could you explain that to me?" Even in difficult situations, we can still demonstrate kindness.

If you enjoy leading children in singing, sing "Must Be Done in Love" (track 6) on the *Moose Mountain: Children's CD.* Lyrics are on page 174.

SUPPLIES & MATERIALS

Kids will need scissors, the Daily Challenge part of this week's student page, and pens or pencils. You'll also need a roll of tape.

THE Daily CHALLENGE

MOOSE TRACKS

If you have younger children or nonreaders, take time to read the Daily Challenges out loud and help them choose one for the coming week. The ideas have pictures beside them to help even nonreaders understand their choices.

You might want to have each child complete this sentence prayer: "Lord, give me courage to challenge _____ this week."

See You Soon

Have each child cut out the Daily Challenge section of his or her student page. Read aloud the Daily Challenge options for this week, then have kids each choose and mark one option they're willing to commit to doing before your next get-together. When each child has chosen an option, show kids how to wrap their Daily Challenges around their wrists and secure them with tape.

SAY: I'm so thankful that ✝ Jesus challenges us. It helps me to have such a great example to follow. Now let's take time to talk to God about what's happening in the lives of our friends.

Have the children share prayer needs in their crews and pray for one another. Then close the time in prayer.

Pray for the kids who are there, thanking God for challenging them and for desiring a relationship with each child. Ask God to help the kids as they challenge others and as they complete their Daily Challenges.

MOOSE MOUNTAIN

GET-TOGETHER

11

Bible Point: **JESUS WANTS TO SPEND TIME WITH US.**

Key Verse: **JAMES 4:8A**

"Come close to God, and God will come close to you."

HOLY BIBLE

JESUS HAS BREAKFAST WITH HIS DISCIPLES.

John 21:1-14

This was the third time Jesus appeared to his disciples after rising from the dead. So it seems they should have known that things had changed—that their lives were going to be different since Jesus had risen from the dead. But instead we find them out fishing, having gone back to their old way of life before they'd met Jesus.

When Jesus caused the fishermen to catch a net full of fish after a night of catching nothing, the miracle made the disciples realize who the man on shore must be. And it also may have reminded them of what Jesus had told them they would be: fishers of men (Matthew 4:19).

Notice that Jesus didn't send out an invitation calling his disciples to a big dinner in his honor. Instead, he went to where they were and began to prepare breakfast himself. Jesus, the risen Son of God, prepared fish and bread for his friends, and he invited them to join him. This was certainly a special time for Jesus' disciples as they sat and ate breakfast with the one who had power not only over fish but also over life and death! Even though Jesus was different somehow—the disciples weren't sure if it was really him—he still wanted to spend time with his followers.

Making It Personal

- Read Matthew 6:6.
- How often do you spend time alone with God?
- Pray: God, as I seek to be more faithful in my time alone with you, please help me to…

A Quick Overview

Activity	Kids will...	You'll need...
WOW!	Begin making homemade ice cream.	*Moose Mountain: Children's CD*, CD player, milk, sugar, vanilla flavoring, ice, rock salt, small and large self-sealing plastic bags, measuring cups, spoons, paper towels
WHAT'S NEW?	Share how they completed their Daily Challenges, and add to the Friendship Chain.	*Moose Mountain: Children's CD*, CD player, bright-colored construction paper, tape, scissors
GRINS & GAMES	Play a game that brings smiles and practices friend making.	Chairs
Getting to Know JESUS	Go "fishing" as they learn about a time Jesus had breakfast with his friends.	*Moose Mountain: Children's CD*, CD player, Bible, yardsticks or dowel rods, string, construction-paper fish, paper clips, tape, magnets
TRY IT OUT!	Enjoy the ice cream they've made, and plan ways to spend time with Jesus.	Get-Together 11 page from *Moose Mountain: For Kids*, pens or pencils, spoons, wet wipes, paper towels
See You Soon	Choose a Daily Challenge to put what they've learned into practice.	Daily Challenges from Get-Together 11 page, pens or pencils, tape, scissors

SUPPLIES & MATERIALS

You'll need milk, sugar, vanilla flavoring, ice, rock salt, small and large self-sealing plastic bags, measuring cups, spoons, paper towels, the *Moose Mountain: Children's CD,* and a CD player.

GO ALL OUT!

Bring in a variety of flavored ice cream syrups or toppings. And don't forget the sprinkles!

FIELD TEST FINDINGS

Name-brand bags work better for this than the cheaper ones. The less expensive bags don't seal as well and allow lots of leaks.

We tried this with both white and chocolate milk. Since the chocolate milk was already sweetened, we didn't add extra sugar. The chocolate ice cream ended up having a little bit of a bitter flavor, so we'd recommend adding the sugar after all.

WOW!

ALLERGY ALERT
See page 12.

Before kids arrive, prepare one self-sealing bag with the following items for each child:

- ½ cup milk
- ¼ teaspoon vanilla flavoring
- 1 tablespoon sugar

Seal each bag securely, and set aside in a chilled location until children begin to arrive.

Turn on the *Moose Mountain: Children's CD,* playing tracks 1-10 to welcome children. As children arrive, let them form pairs and begin making ice cream together. Each pair will take two of the bags you prepared before class and gently place them inside a larger self-sealing plastic bag. Then help each pair add enough ice to fill the larger bag halfway and top this with ½ cup of rock salt. Have children seal the bag and work together, gently massaging the larger bag with their two smaller bags inside.

Remind children to be gentle in their squeezing and smushing so they don't break open the bags of milk.

Continue this until each child has found a partner and prepared a larger bag. Have a helper or older child prepare an extra bag or two for latecomers.

When you're ready to begin, have kids set their bags aside and move to the next activity.

FIELD TEST FINDINGS

Yes, this activity really works! The kids were so excited about making their own bags of ice cream. Since this snack takes a long time to prepare, it clearly ties in with the point of the lesson!

This is a wet snack to prepare, so be sure you have *plenty* of towels or paper towels on hand. Or you can prepare this outdoors if the weather is not too hot (it's hard for the ice cream to set on blazing days and when kids place their bags of ice on a hot sidewalk).

SOMETIMES MY MOOSCLES COME IN HANDY!

SUPPLIES & MATERIALS

You'll need bright-colored construction paper, tape, scissors, the *Moose Mountain: Children's CD,* and a CD player.

WHAT'S NEW?

When everyone has arrived, have kids and leaders circle up with their crews, sitting knee-to-knee so conversation will be easier. Help any newcomers find crews. Give kids a chance to shake hands and introduce themselves to anyone new in the crews.

SAY: Last week we each chose a Daily Challenge to complete to show our friendship with Jesus. Let's take a minute or two now to see how that went!

Choose two or three kids or leaders to tell which Daily Challenge they picked and what happened when they carried it out. Then have everyone share in his or her crew so each Daily Challenge is heard. Softly play tracks 9-10 on the *Moose Mountain: Children's CD* while children share.

SAY: We want to celebrate the growth of our friendship with Jesus and with others, so each week we're adding links to a Friendship Chain.

Point out the progress made on the Friendship Chain last week, then have each child who completed a Daily Challenge add one link to the chain. If you have several crews, help them work together as they attach their last links so the chains for each crew are joined into one chain. Then add this to the big Friendship Chain. Turn off the music, then have leaders put aside the supplies and hold up the chain.

SAY: The love and friendship of Jesus is really growing around here! Now let's play a fun game that will help us learn more about the kind of friend Jesus is.

GRINS & GAMES

Have kids take a quick break before the game and return to squishing their ice cream bags. Let them do this for about two minutes, then turn their attention back to you for the game.

Have kids put the chairs in a circle and sit in them. You'll need one chair per person, not including you.

Stand in the center of the circle and **SAY:** I'm going to tell you something I like to do with my friends. If you like to do that too, you'll stand up and quickly find another chair to sit in. I'll try to find a chair to sit in while everyone is moving around! Begin the game by naming an activity you enjoy doing with your friends that kids are also likely to enjoy, such as going to the movies or going out for ice cream. Find a chair as kids who also enjoy this activity move to different chairs. This will leave one person in the center of the circle. Have this person say something he or she enjoys doing with friends. Continue the game as long as time allows.

When the game is over, **ASK:**

- Did we forget anything? Are there any other things friends like to do together?

SAY: Even the most boring activity can be fun if you have a friend with you. Friends like to spend time together!  Jesus wants to spend time with us, too! Let's look in the Bible to find out more about this.

SUPPLIES & MATERIALS

You'll need chairs.

MOOSE TRACKS

No chairs? Give each person a piece of construction paper or section of newsprint to place on the floor and sit on. During the game, kids can only sit on available pieces of paper.

SUPPLIES & MATERIALS

You'll need the *Moose Mountain: Children's CD,* a CD player, a Bible, yardsticks or dowel rods, string, construction-paper fish, paper clips, tape, and magnets.

MOOSE TRACKS

If you have older kids, you can have them each cut out one or two fish shapes themselves instead of doing this ahead of time.

Before kids arrive, cut out a bunch of fish shapes from construction paper. You can use the pattern on page 171 as a guide. Attach a paper clip to the mouth area of each fish. Prepare one fishing pole for each crew by tying string to the end of a yardstick or dowel.

Have kids take a quick break before the activity and return to squishing their ice cream bags. Let them do this for about two minutes, then turn their attention back to you for the Bible story.

Have each crew sit in a circle. If you only have two crews, form one large circle. Give each crew a fishing pole and a few fish to place in a pile on the floor in the middle of the circle.

Hold up your Bible and **SAY:** We're going to hear a story from the Bible. As you listen, I want you to take turns fishing for the fish in the center of your circle. Toss the end of your line in, and try to snag a fish.

Kids may complain that this won't work since there's no hook on the line. Just brush aside their comments and tell them to try. Then play "Gone Fishing, Part 1" (track 15) on the CD.

After the track is over, stop the CD and **ASK:**

• What has your fishing experience been like so far today?
• How do you think the disciples felt after fishing all night without catching anything?

SAY: Before we find out what happened to Jesus' friends, let's make an improvement to the fishing rods.

Give each crew a small magnet and some tape. Have kids tape the magnets to the end of the string.

Then play "Gone Fishing, Part 2" (track 16) on the CD as kids begin to "fish" again. When the track is over, stop the CD and **ASK:**

- How did your fishing experience change?
- How is this like what happened to Jesus' friends?
- How do you think they felt when they realized it was Jesus on the shore?
- What do you think they talked about during breakfast?
- What are other times you can think of when Jesus hung out with his friends?
- Why do you think they spent so much time together?

SAY: Over the past weeks, we've looked at a lot of examples from Jesus' life. The breakfast on the shore is just one of many, many times Jesus enjoyed being with his friends. It seems like Jesus was almost always spending time with his disciples!

✝ Jesus wants to spend time with us, too.

I'M GLAD YOU LIKE TO SPEND TIME WITH ME, ROOFUS. LET'S GO OUT TO BREAKFAST TOMORROW— I'LL EVEN LET YOU PICK THE PLACE.

LET'S GO GET CINNAMON ROLLS AND HOT CHOCOLATE. THEY MATCH MY FURRY COAT, SO SPILLS WON'T SHOW.

SUPPLIES & MATERIALS

Kids will need the "Time for Jesus" section of the Get-Together 11 page from their *Moose Mountain: For Kids* books and pens or pencils. You'll also need spoons, paper towels, and wet wipes.

CD-ROM

MOOSE TRACKS

If you enjoy leading kids in singing, try "Praise Him" (track 8) on the *Moose Mountain: Children's CD.* Lyrics are on page 174.

FIELD TEST FINDINGS

Be sure to tell kids to dump out the bags of ice water in a designated area (outdoors or in a sink). We had a few spills before we made this announcement!

TRY IT OUT!

ALLERGY ALERT
See page 12.

Announce that it's time to eat the ice cream! Have kids clean their hands at a nearby sink or with wet wipes, then demonstrate how to carefully open the larger bag without dumping out the contents. Show kids how to lift out the bags of ice cream and carefully wipe off the tops with paper towels to remove the salt water (otherwise the salt will get into the ice cream). Then let the kids dig in and eat right out of their bags!

As kids are eating, comment that making ice cream takes a lot of time and effort. **ASK:**

- **Is homemade ice cream worth the time and effort it takes to make it? Why or why not?**
- **Are friendships worth the time and effort they take? Why or why not?**
- **What kind of time does a friendship take?**
- **What kind of effort does a friendship take?**
- **Is a friendship with Jesus worth time and effort? Why or why not?**
- **Our verse is** James 4:8, **which says, "Come close to God, and God will come close to you." What do you think this means?**

SAY: Let's think of ways we can spend time with Jesus this week.

Have kids look at the "Time for Jesus" section of their student page. Point out the sections of the "clock" and the areas where kids can write or draw ideas for spending time with Jesus. For example, kids might write "sing songs to Jesus" in the "In the Car" area. Have them work together in their crews, brainstorming ideas and filling in the areas. Each child's clock may be different, but kids can glean ideas from one another. Encourage kids to take these home and place them near their clocks so they'll be reminded regularly of ways they can spend time with Jesus.

When children have finished their clocks, **SAY:** Let's get our Daily Challenges ready so we can continue to put this into practice this week!

Have each child cut out the Daily Challenge section of his or her student page. Read aloud the Daily Challenge options for this week, then have kids each choose and mark one option they're willing to commit to doing before your next get-together. When each child has chosen an option, show kids how to wrap their Daily Challenges around their wrists and secure them with tape.

SAY: I'm so thankful that ✝ Jesus wants to spend time with us. It helps me to have such a great example to follow. Now let's take time to talk to God about what's happening in the lives of our friends.

Have the children share prayer needs in their crews and pray for one another. Then close the time in prayer.

Pray for the kids who are there, thanking God for wanting to spend time with them and for desiring a relationship with each child. Ask God to help the kids as they spend time with others and as they complete their Daily Challenges.

MORE TIME FOR FUN?

If you still have time, let kids work in their crews to complete the back side of their student page. Encourage kids to share their responses and thoughts with others in their crews. If kids don't have time to finish these reflections on the get-together, encourage them to take time at home this week to do so.

SUPPLIES & MATERIALS

Kids will need scissors, the Daily Challenge part of this week's student page, and pens or pencils. You'll also need a roll of tape.

THE Daily CHALLENGE

MOOSE TRACKS

If you have younger children or nonreaders, take time to read the Daily Challenges out loud and help them choose one for the coming week. The ideas have pictures beside them to help even nonreaders understand their choices.

You may want to have children complete this sentence prayer, filling in a place or activity: "Jesus, help me to spend more time with you when I'm _____."

MOOSE MOUNTAIN

12

Bible Point: **JESUS KEEPS HIS PROMISES.**

Key Verse: **PSALM 145:13B**

"The Lord always keeps his promises; he is gracious in all he does."

HOLY
BIBLE

HOLY BIBLE

Bible
BACKGROUND
FOR LEADERS

JESUS APPEARS TO HIS DISCIPLES.

Mark 10:33-34; Luke 24:35-49

Mark 10:33-34 describes the third time Jesus talked about his coming death and resurrection. The first time, described in Mark 8:31-33, Peter rebuked Jesus, not wanting to hear such talk, and Jesus confronted Peter about this. Apparently Peter learned his lesson because we read of no opposition this time.

These descriptions of what was to come were not vague suggestions that anyone could predict. This passage clearly states where things would happen, who would accuse and condemn Jesus, and who would torture and execute him. Both descriptions also mention Jesus' coming resurrection. In effect, Jesus promised that after he died, he would rise from the dead.

In Luke 24, we see that what Jesus predicted actually took place. It's interesting to note that even after the accurate prediction of Jesus' rejection and crucifixion, the disciples still seemed skeptical about Jesus' resurrection. Even when he showed his hands and feet and offered to let the disciples touch him, they still couldn't fully believe. His request for something to eat was likely another attempt to prove to them that he was real and not just a ghost. Jesus had fulfilled his prediction and kept his promise. He truly was alive in a glorified body, and even though it seemed too good to believe, the disciples eventually understood and received Jesus' commission to continue spreading the word about the forgiveness available to all through Jesus.

Making It Personal

- Read Revelation 22:6.
- What promises of God should you be trusting for your future?
- Pray: Lord, help me to demonstrate my trust in you as I…

A Quick Overview

Activity	Kids will...	You'll need...
WOW!	Experiment with illusions and sleight-of-hand tricks.	Aromatic or attractive snack, supplies for illusions you choose based on the options
WHAT'S NEW?	Share how they completed their Daily Challenges, and add to the Friendship Chain.	*Moose Mountain: Children's CD*, CD player, bright-colored construction paper, tape, scissors
GRINS & GAMES	Play a game that brings smiles and practices friend making.	Adult or teen volunteer
Getting to Know JESUS	Compare a promise Jesus made to his actions.	Bibles, paper, pens or pencils
TRY IT OUT!	Help you keep a promise!	Snack you prepared before class, wet wipes, saltine crackers
See You Soon	Choose a Daily Challenge to put what they've learned into practice.	Get-Together 12 page from *Moose Mountain: For Kids*, pens or pencils, tape, scissors

I PROMISE WE'RE GOING TO HAVE FUN TODAY!

SUPPLIES & MATERIALS

You'll need an aromatic or visually appealing snack, such as freshly baked cinnamon buns, warm cookies, or a tray of frosted doughnuts. You'll also need the supplies for the illusions you choose.

MOOSE TRACKS

Warm baked goods smell so wonderful! If you can, bake your treats at your church or meeting place so you can bring them into the classroom piping hot.

FIELD TEST FINDINGS

This one is tricky for younger kids who can't figure years and numbers, but it worked great with the older ones.

146

WOW!

Set the snack item where kids can see it. If they comment on it, assure them that they'll have it for snack later.

In this experience, kids will have the opportunity to observe and learn a few illusions or sleight-of-hand tricks. We've provided two simple tricks you can do yourself and teach kids. You can also purchase a variety of simple illusions at a local store or online, or you can create cheesy illusions, such as making your leg "disappear" behind a towel and then reappear when you take the towel away.

If you purchase illusions, set these out and invite children to try them as they enter the room. Or read the directions yourself and then perform the tricks for children as they enter. Teach them to do the tricks so they can perform them for kids who arrive next.

Here are two illusions you can use as kids arrive. Again, perform them for the kids first, then assist them in doing the tricks for those who arrive next. If you have time, you might check out a book of illusions or sleight-of-hand tricks from a local library and add to your repertoire!

ILLUSION 1

Before kids arrive, write a number on a piece of paper, and seal it inside an envelope. The number should be the current year doubled. For example, if the year is 2009, the number you write should be 2018.

Give a child a piece of paper and pencil. Ask the child to write the year he or she was born. Then ask the child to write the year he or she learned to swim (or started school, learned to ride a bike, first came to your church, or any other memorable event). Then ask the child to write the number of years that have passed since this event. Finally, ask the child to write his or her age. Provide a calculator so the child can quickly tally these numbers. When the child has the sum, let him or her open the sealed envelope—the numbers will match! Or, if the child has already had a birthday that year, the number will be off by one—still pretty close!

How does it work? It's a simple matter of addition. The year a child is born plus his or her age will equal the current year. The year a child experienced the significant event plus the number of years since that will equal the current year again. Add these for double the current year.

ILLUSION 2

Ask a child what his or her favorite number between 1 and 10 is. Write this number on a sugar cube with a pencil. Hold the cube between your thumb and index finger so your fingertip touches the number. Drop the cube into a cup of water, and ask the child to stir the water. Then hold the child's hand over the cup and say, "I can make your number reappear!" Take away your hand, and the number will appear on the child's hand!

How does it work? The pencil lead on your fingertip will easily transfer to the child's hand. Just be sure no one sees your fingertip! This is an easy one for kids to try and master right away.

Kids may offer knowledge of other tricks they've learned or seen performed. See if together you can think of ways illusionists pull off their tricks and fool us into believing they've really made something disappear (or whatever the trick may be). Ask kids how they feel about being tricked into believing what the illusionist claims is true—even when they know it can't be.

GO ALL OUT!

Invite an illusionist from your church or community to do a few tricks for your group. Most won't be willing to give up their secrets, but ask your illusionist ahead of time if he or she would be willing to perform and then teach a simple illusion to your class.

FIELD TEST FINDINGS

We tried some funny ones such as making fingers "leap" from one hand to another. Simply hold up two of your left-hand fingers, explain that you're going to transfer them to your right hand, and on the count of three, pop up two fingers on your right hand while closing your left hand into a fist. Goofy? Yes! But even the older kids were laughing.

HOW'D THEY
DO THAT?

SUPPLIES & MATERIALS

You'll need bright-colored construction paper, tape, scissors, the *Moose Mountain: Children's CD*, and a CD player.

MOOSE TRACKS

By now your Friendship Chain will be really long! Consider a way to celebrate the growth children have experienced and demonstrated by the last get-together. Perhaps you can invite parents and other adults to visit your classroom and let kids tell about the Friendship Chain. Or hang it in a place highly visible to adults with a poster telling how the chain was created.

FIELD TEST FINDINGS

By now our field test Friendship Chain was just a foot or two from going around the edge of the entire room. The challenge was to make it all the way around by the last get-together!

When everyone has arrived, put aside the illusion supplies. Have kids and leaders circle up with their crews, sitting knee-to-knee so conversation will be easier. Help any newcomers find crews. Give kids a chance to shake hands and introduce themselves to anyone new in the crews.

SAY: Last week we each chose a Daily Challenge to complete to show our friendship with Jesus. Let's take a minute or two now to see how that went!

Choose two or three kids or leaders to tell which Daily Challenge they picked and what happened when they carried it out. Then have everyone share in his or her crew so each Daily Challenge is heard. Softly play "Standing on the Promises" (track 7) on the *Moose Mountain: Children's CD* while children share.

SAY: We want to celebrate the growth of our friendship with Jesus and with others, so each week we're adding links to a Friendship Chain.

Point out the progress made on the Friendship Chain last week, then have each child who completed a Daily Challenge add one link to the chain. If you have several crews, help them work together as they attach their last links so the chains for each crew are joined into one chain. Then add this to the big Friendship Chain. Turn off the music, then have leaders put aside the supplies and hold up the chain.

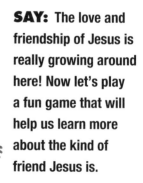

SAY: The love and friendship of Jesus is really growing around here! Now let's play a fun game that will help us learn more about the kind of friend Jesus is.

Introduce your volunteer. **SAY:** **Did you know that this person has the special ability to untie difficult knots?** Cue your volunteer to nod in agreement as if he or she was an expert on knots. [Name of volunteer] **is going to demonstrate this ability right now!** Cue your volunteer to respond, "I can untie any knot you make!"

Have kids hold hands and form one large circle. Explain that you want kids to get themselves into a great big tangle. Have your volunteer turn his or her back while kids mix their circle into a large knot. They might step over others' linking hands, turn part of the circle inside out, and so on. You might want to assist kids with this so they make a great big knot.

When they're ready, turn your volunteer around, and allow him or her to start untangling the knot. Have the volunteer begin by making comments about how easy this will be. Then the volunteer should start making comments about how difficult it is and talk about something silly he or she really needs to leave to do. He or she can say, "I don't know if I have time for this anyway. I've got to get home to watch TV." Finally, your volunteer should give up and say something like, "I just can't do it!"

Have kids return to their crews and sit down. **SAY:** [Name of volunteer] **promised to untangle your knot. But our volunteer didn't keep that promise. In your crews, talk about how it feels when someone makes a promise and then breaks it.**

Allow a few minutes for discussion, then **SAY:** **It's disappointing when someone doesn't keep a promise. It makes us feel let down and unimportant. Today we're learning that**  **Jesus keeps his promises. Let's find out how.**

SUPPLIES & MATERIALS

You'll need an adult or teen volunteer who's been cued ahead of time about how to respond in this activity.

MOOSE TRACKS

Be sure to clear tables and chairs out of the way when playing this game!

If you enjoy leading children in singing, sing "Standing on the Promises" (track 7) on the *Moose Mountain: Children's CD*. Lyrics are on page 174.

SUPPLIES & MATERIALS

You'll need Bibles, paper, and pens or pencils.

MOOSE TRACKS

If you have crews with children who don't read, have the crew leaders read aloud and take notes on what children discuss.

Getting to Know JESUS

SAY: We're going to look in the Bible for a promise Jesus made and then see if he kept this promise.

Be sure each crew has a Bible, paper, and pen or pencil. Have crews turn to Mark 10:33-34.

SAY: Read your passage aloud in your crew and look for a promise Jesus made. Then put this in your own words. Explain it so anyone your age could understand it. Have one person in your crew take notes so you can report your findings.

When crews have finished, let them do the same thing with Luke 24:35-49. This time they should be looking for proof that Jesus *kept* his promise.

Allow several minutes for crews to work together and discuss, then **ASK:**

• **What promise did Jesus make?**

When children from several crews have responded, **SAY:** In this Scripture, Jesus referred to himself as the "Son of Man" and promised that even though he would be killed, he would rise again after three days. That's a pretty big promise! Let's find out what happened.

Allow someone to report what his or her crew discussed about the second passage. Then ask:

• **How did Jesus keep his promise?**

When children have responded, **SAY:** The Bible tells us that Jesus died on the cross and came back to life three days later. Jesus wanted to make sure his friends knew that what he had promised had really happened. He appeared to them, let them touch him, and ate with them. He kept this amazing promise! **ASK:**

- What do you think Jesus' friends thought when he made this promise?
- What do you think they were feeling when they realized Jesus had kept his amazing promise?
- Why was it important for Jesus to keep his promise?
- Why is it important for us to keep our promises?

SAY: 📖 Jesus keeps his promises. He promised he would die and come back to life, and he did it! Earlier today we did some fun tricks and illusions. We wanted to fool people into believing we could do something amazing or impossible. When we see an illusion, we know we're being tricked, even if we don't know how the trick is done. We know a tiger isn't really disappearing. We know a person isn't really being sawed in half. Those are tricks. But Jesus didn't trick us. He didn't fool us into believing something that wasn't true. He really kept his promise!

I THINK HE USED A SAW...

I REMEMBER WHEN WE WENT TO SEE THE AMAZING HOOT-DINI. HE SAWED A TREE IN HALF! I WONDER HOW HE DID THAT!

SUPPLIES & MATERIALS

You'll need the snack you prepared before class, wet wipes, and a box of saltine crackers.

MOOSE TRACKS

If you have time, lead kids in the knotted bracelet activity on their student page. Otherwise, send this home with kids, and tell them they can make the bracelets as further reminders that friends keep their promises.

ALLERGY ALERT
See page 12.

Have children clean their hands with wet wipes or at a nearby sink.

SAY: Our Bible verse is 💟 Psalm 145:13b, and it says, "The Lord always keeps his promises; he is gracious in all he does." What's the big deal about keeping promises? Why is that so important? Let kids respond. As they're sharing, begin handing out saltines. The kids are sure to protest that you said they could have the wonderful-smelling baked snack. When they do, say: **I was going to give you that, but now I'm thinking of saving it for myself. These crackers will be a good snack for you. Won't that be OK?** Kids will again protest. **ASK:**

• **So if I give you crackers instead of the snack you were expecting, am I keeping my promise?**

When kids respond, bring out the baked treat, assure kids that they can trust you to keep your promises, and serve the treat to the kids. As they eat, **ASK:**

• **How does it feel when someone *does* keep a promise?**

• **Every time we've been together, I've given you a good snack. Does that seem like a promise to give you a good snack again today? Why or why not?**

• **When is it hard to keep a promise? easy to keep one?**

SAY: Even when it's hard, we need to do our very best to keep our promises. Or we simply shouldn't make promises that we can't keep. We know how much we count on others to keep their promises. I'm especially glad that ✝ Jesus keeps his promises!

See You Soon

Have each child cut out the Daily Challenge section of his or her student page. Read aloud the Daily Challenge options for this week, then have kids each choose and mark one option they're willing to commit to doing before your next get-together. When each child has chosen an option, show kids how to wrap their Daily Challenges around their wrists and secure them with tape.

SAY: I'm so thankful that ✝ Jesus keeps his promises. It helps me to have such a great example to follow. Now let's take time to talk to God about what's happening in the lives of our friends.

Have the children share prayer needs in their crews and pray for one another. Then close the time in prayer.

Pray for the kids who are there, thanking God for keeping his promises to them and for desiring a relationship with each child. Ask God to help the kids as they keep their promises to others and as they complete their Daily Challenges.

MORE TIME FOR FUN?

If you still have time, let kids work in their crews to complete the back side of their student page. Encourage kids to share their responses and thoughts with others in their crews. If kids don't have time to finish these reflections on the get-together, encourage them to take time at home this week to do so.

SUPPLIES & MATERIALS

Kids will need scissors, the Daily Challenge part of this week's student page, and pens or pencils. You'll also need a roll of tape.

THE Daily CHALLENGE

MOOSE TRACKS

If you have younger children or nonreaders, take time to read the Daily Challenges out loud and help them choose one for the coming week. The ideas have pictures beside them to help even nonreaders understand their choices.

You might want to have children complete this sentence prayer: "Jesus, help me keep my promise to _____."

GET-TOGETHER

13

Bible Point: **JESUS IS ALWAYS WITH US.**

Key Verse: **MATTHEW 28:20b**

"And be sure of this: I am with you always, even to the end of the age."

JESUS GIVES THE GREAT COMMISSION.
Matthew 28:16-20; Acts 1:1-11

In Matthew 28, Jesus placed the future of all he had done on earth into the hands of his disciples. He commissioned them with a task that has yet to be completely fulfilled: "Go and make disciples of all the nations." As Christians we have inherited that commission to reach our world for Christ today. But Jesus didn't just give a task; he promised support. He told them, and us, that he would be with his people always, even to the end of the world as we know it!

Before Jesus physically departed for heaven, he gave his followers a plan for reaching the world. First they were to wait. The power would come when the Holy Spirit came upon them. Then they were to move out from Jerusalem step by step, eventually reaching the ends of the earth. That plan is a good one for us to follow as well. If we have the Holy Spirit in our lives, he'll empower us to reach others for Christ, whether they're across the street or across the world.

As Jesus was ascending into heaven, angels came to give the disciples one last prod and one last promise. It did no good for the followers to stand looking into the sky. They needed to get going on the plan Jesus had laid out for them. The promise the angels gave was that Jesus would return—in a powerful and unanticipated way—as he had departed from them.

Making It Personal

- Read Matthew 28:19-20.
- Imagine Jesus personally inviting you to carry out his plans! How do his words make you feel?
- Pray: Lord, please build my confidence and strengthen my desire to participate in your awesome work. Help me with the doubts I have about…

A Quick Overview

Activity	Kids will...	You'll need...
WOW!	Play with a variety of round or circle-shaped toys.	*Moose Mountain: Children's CD*, CD player, variety of balls, Hula Hoops, yo-yos, spinning tops
WHAT'S NEW?	Share how they completed their Daily Challenges, and add to the Friendship Chain.	Bright-colored construction paper, tape, scissors
GRINS & GAMES	Do experiments that bring smiles and practice friend making.	Balloons, metallic confetti, ball
Getting to Know JESUS	Participate in a drama based on the Great Commission.	*Moose Mountain: Children's CD*, CD player, Bible
TRY IT OUT!	Enjoy a snack, and make plans to keep in touch with friends.	Bagels; variety of toppings such as cream cheese, butter, and jelly; wet wipes; paper plates; plastic knives; Get-Together 13 page from *Moose Mountain: For Kids*; pens or pencils
See You Soon	Choose a Daily Challenge to put what they've learned into practice.	Daily Challenges from Get-Together 13 page, pens or pencils, tape, small bouncy balls, scissors

SUPPLIES & MATERIALS

You'll need the *Moose Mountain: Children's CD,* a CD player, and a variety of balls, Hula Hoops, yo-yos, and spinning tops.

WOW!

Before kids arrive, turn on the CD and play tracks 1-10. Repeat these tracks to provide fun and welcoming music as kids arrive.

As kids enter the room, let them play with the toys. See if kids can create games using the items. For example, kids might toss balls through a hoop, see if they can get all the tops spinning at the same time, create tricks with the yo-yos, and so on. Let them be creative and have fun with the toys.

FIELD TEST FINDINGS

The kids in our field test invented some fun games! One involved trying to toss a ball through a Hula Hoop while another child actually used the Hula Hoop. Another crew invented a variation of "hot potato" that required everyone to pass a ball quickly while one child used a yo-yo. When the person with the yo-yo made a mistake and couldn't get the yo-yo back into his or her hand, the child holding the ball became the new yo-yo spinner.

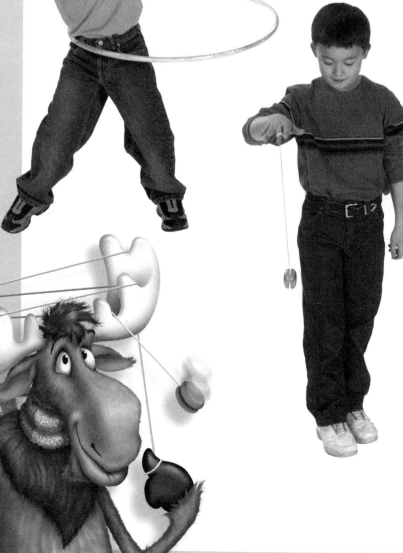

When everyone has arrived, put aside the toys. Have kids and leaders circle up with their crews, sitting knee-to-knee so conversation will be easier. Help any newcomers find crews. Give kids a chance to shake hands and introduce themselves to anyone new in the crews.

SAY: Last week we each chose a Daily Challenge to complete to show our friendship with Jesus. Let's take a minute or two now to see how that went!

Choose two or three kids or leaders to tell which Daily Challenge they picked and what happened when they carried it out. Then have everyone share in his or her crew so each Daily Challenge is heard.

SAY: We want to celebrate the growth of our friendship with Jesus and with others, so each week we're adding links to a Friendship Chain.

Point out the progress made on the Friendship Chain last week, then have each child who completed a Daily Challenge add one link to the chain. If you have several crews, help them work together as they attach their last links so the chains for each crew are joined into one chain. Then add this to the big Friendship Chain. Have leaders put aside the supplies, and have each child take a part of the chain so you are all holding it together.

SUPPLIES & MATERIALS

You'll need bright-colored construction paper, tape, and scissors.

FIELD TEST FINDINGS

By this final get-together, our field test group's Friendship Chain went all the way around the room—and then some! This prayer activity was a great celebration of what kids had learned and what they'd done to show Jesus' love. They wanted to hang the chain from the ceiling and keep it as a reminder of our get-togethers.

What's New? Continued...

SAY: The love and friendship of Jesus has grown so much over the past weeks! It's amazing to see this chain and know that friendships have grown because of your choices and actions! Let's thank God for the friendships he's grown in our get-togethers.

Pray this prayer, filling in the blank with one thing you've learned about Jesus during the Moose Mountain get-togethers: **Jesus, thank you that you are _____.** Then have the child to your left pray, then the next child, and so on around the chain until everyone has prayed. Close the prayer by thanking God for everything the kids have done through their Daily Challenges to demonstrate the love and friendship of Jesus.

SAY: Now let's do a few fun activities that will help us learn even more about the kind of friend Jesus is!

You'll need balloons, metallic confetti, and a ball.

Have one person in each crew inflate and tie off a balloon. Younger kids may need leaders to help them or do this step for them. Demonstrate how to rub the inflated balloon against your hair to build up static electricity. Have each crew do this with its balloon.

Give each crew a handful of metallic confetti to sprinkle on the floor or table where the crew is gathered. Ask kids to predict what will happen if the balloon gets close to the confetti, then let them hold their balloons near the confetti and see what happens.
ASK:

• **Were you surprised when the confetti stuck to the balloon? Why or why not?**
• **How does the confetti stick to the balloon?**

SAY: This experiment works because of static electricity. This is a kind of energy that is around us, but we can't see it. When you rubbed the balloons on your hair, you collected a bunch of static electricity, and it made the confetti stick! Even though we can't see static electricity, we can see what it does. Let's try another experiment.

MOOSE TRACKS

Larger latex balloons are easier to inflate than tiny water balloons.

Ask kids to take a big breath and then to hold their breath. As they're puffed up and trying not to breathe, **SAY:** Don't answer this question out loud since you can't talk and hold your breath at the same time. How do you know there will still be air around you when you're ready to take a breath? Let kids get a breath of air, then have them answer the question you asked. **ASK:**

• **What would happen if no air was available?**

After they've responded, **SAY:** Air is all around us. We can't see it, but we trust that it's there! Let's do one more experiment.

Hold up the ball and **ASK:**

• **What will happen when I let go of this ball?** Let kids respond, then drop the ball to see if they were correct. **ASK:**
• **How did you know the ball would fall to the ground?**

MOOSE TRACKS

If you enjoy leading kids in singing, use "What a Friend We Have in Jesus" (track 2) on the *Moose Mountain: Children's CD*. Lyrics are on page 172.

Grins & Games Continued...

Let kids respond, then **SAY:** Even though we can't see gravity, it's always with us. It keeps our feet on the ground, along with everything else! So what do static electricity, air, and gravity all have in common? Let kids respond, then say: We can't see any of these, but they're always there. The same is true of Jesus! Even though we can't see him, ✝ Jesus is always with us. Let's check out what the Bible says about this.

IF I DO THAT EXPERIMENT, I'LL GET CONFETTI ALL OVER MY FURRY BROWN COAT.

DON'T WORRY, ROOFUS. I'VE GOT ANTI-CLING SPRAY IN MY PURSE. I'LL SPRAY THE CONFETTI FOR YOU.

Getting to Know
JESUS

SUPPLIES & MATERIALS

You'll need the *Moose Mountain: Children's CD,* a CD player, and a Bible.

Show kids your Bible and **SAY:** The Bible tells us in Matthew and Acts about Jesus' last moments here on earth. Let's act out a fun drama that will give us an idea of what happened the last time Jesus was with his friends.

Explain that all the kids (and leaders!) will play the parts of the disciples. They will listen to the directions "Coach Jesus" gives them and respond accordingly. Play "Coach Jesus" (track 17) on the *Moose Mountain: Children's CD,* and participate with the kids. When the track is over, turn off the CD and have kids return to their seats.

SAY: In the Bible, Jesus didn't really act like a soccer coach, but he did tell his friends what he wanted them to do and what they should expect in the coming days. Let's look in our Bibles at exactly what happened.

Have half the crews look up and read Matthew 28:16-20 and the other half look up and read Acts 1:1-11. Then have a reporter from each crew tell one thing his or her crew noticed or learned in that passage. **ASK:**

• What did Jesus want his friends to do?
• Why was this important?
• What promises did Jesus make to his friends?
• Why were these promises important?

Getting to Know Jesus Continued...

SAY: Our verse today comes from the passage in Matthew. It's Matthew 28:20b, and it says, "And be sure of this: I am with you always, even to the end of the age." **ASK:**

• What does it mean to you to know that [✝] Jesus is always with us?

• How do our examples of air, gravity, and static electricity remind you that [✝] Jesus is always with us?

• Think back to the toys we played with at the beginning of our get-together. How could these remind you that [✝] Jesus is always with us?

SAY: All of the toys we played with were round—without beginning or end. A circle or ball can be a symbol of forever because it never ends. When we see a ball or a circle, we can remember that [✝] Jesus is always with us, forever and ever and ever...Well, you get the idea! We can't always be with our friends, but we can be so committed to our friends that we stick with them for years and years and years. Let's have a snack as we keep on thinking about this idea.

ALLERGY ALERT
See page 12.

Have children clean their hands with wet wipes or at a nearby sink. Then set out the bagels and toppings. Let kids build their own bagel creations, choosing the toppings they prefer.

Have kids return to their crews to eat their snacks. While they eat, **ASK:**

- **How does the shape of our snack remind you that  Jesus is always with us?**
- **Which friend have you had the longest?**
- **What has helped you and that friend stay friends for such a long time?**
- **What things help friends stick together for years and years?**

SAY: Over the past weeks, we've learned from the example of Jesus about a lot of ways friends treat each other. We've learned that friends listen, are kind, are accepting, are trusting, and more! We've all grown in our friendships! Let's be sure to keep these friendships growing.

Have kids use the "Let's Stay Together!" section of their student page to share and record contact information with others in their crews. Encourage leaders to participate so kids can stay in touch with them as well.

SAY: You can call each other, send each other notes, or e-mail—just keep your friendships alive and growing!

SUPPLIES & MATERIALS

You'll need bagels; a variety of toppings such as cream cheese, butter, and jelly; wet wipes; paper plates; and plastic knives. Kids will also need pens or pencils and the "Let's Stay Together!" section of the Get-Together 13 page from their *Moose Mountain: For Kids* books.

CD-ROM

MOOSE TRACKS

For safety purposes, cut the bagels in half before kids arrive. Or purchase presliced bagels.

Now's the perfect time to invite kids to join other programs your church offers, such as Sunday school, midweek, or children's church.

GO ALL OUT!

Provide a variety of bagel flavors, such as berry, honey, and chocolate chip. Kids tend to like sweet and fruit-flavored bagels more than garlic or herb-flavored ones. What else can you put on a bagel? Chocolate chips? Sprinkles? Whipped cream? Let your imagination run wild, and give kids a super tasty snack!

SUPPLIES & MATERIALS

Kids will need scissors, the Daily Challenge part of this week's student page, and pens or pencils. You'll also need a small bouncy ball for each child and a roll of tape.

THE *Daily* CHALLENGE

GO ALL OUT!

Turn this time into an autograph party! Instead of small bouncy balls, give each child a larger plastic ball (the colorful kind you see in big bins at toy stores that cost about $1 or less) and a permanent marker. Turn on any of the songs (tracks 1-10) from the *Moose Mountain: Children's CD,* and let kids write notes of encouragement and sign their names on the other balls. Be sure each person writes his or her own name on the ball so they don't get mixed up.

See You Soon

SAY: As we finish our get-togethers, I want each of you to have a reminder of the friendship we have with Jesus and the friendships we can have with each other.

Give each child a bouncy ball, and thank kids for joining you in this fun time of friendship.

SAY: And we can still do Daily Challenges to keep on growing in friendship!

Have each child cut out the Daily Challenge section of his or her student page. Read aloud the Daily Challenge options for this week, then have kids each choose and mark one option they're willing to commit to doing. When each child has chosen an

GET YOUR ELLIE AUTOGRAPHS HERE!

DOES ANYONE WANT MY AUTOGRAPH?

option, show kids how to wrap their Daily Challenges around their wrists and secure them with tape.

SAY: I'm so thankful that 📖 Jesus is always with us. Now let's take time to talk to God about what's happening in the lives of our friends.

Have the children share prayer needs in their crews and pray for each other. Then close the time in prayer.

Pray for the kids who are there, thanking God for being with them and for desiring a relationship with each child. Ask God to help the kids as they demonstrate love to others and as they complete their Daily Challenges.

MORE TIME FOR FUN?

If you still have time, let kids work in their crews to complete the back side of their student page. Encourage kids to share their responses and thoughts with others in their crews. If kids don't have time to finish these reflections on the get-together, encourage them to take time at home this week to do so.

If you have younger children or nonreaders, take time to read the Daily Challenges out loud and help them choose one for the coming week. The ideas have pictures beside them to help even nonreaders understand their choices.

You might want to have children complete this sentence prayer: "Jesus, thank you that you're always with me. Help me to have courage when I _____ because you're there."

MOOSE MOUNTAIN

PHOTOCOPIABLE PAGES

YOU CAN PRINT THESE PAGES FROM THE PRINTABLE PAGES SECTION ON THE MOOSE MOUNTAIN: FOR KIDS CD-ROM.

Your Mission

Cut out the sections below, and put each one in an envelope.

 Your mission is to smile for at least five people. Get started now!

 Your mission is to shake hands with at least five people. Get started now!

 Your mission is to give high-fives to at least five people. Get started now!

 Your mission is to help serve the snack. Be ready!

 Your mission is to say something nice to three people. Get started now!

I LIKE YOU!

YOU'RE FUN!

 Your mission is to thank a leader for being here today.

THANKS! YOU ARE A GREAT LEADER!

FISH PATTERNS

I Will Be Your Friend

When you're up, when you're down,
When you smile, when you frown,
I will help you get through.
I will be there for you.

Chorus 1

I will be your friend.
I will be your friend.
You've got me and I've got you. Yes, it's true
'Cause I, I will be your friend.
I will be your friend.

When you're feelin' mighty blue,
When you don't know what to do,
Just pray to God. He'll bring you through
'Cause he will be there for you.

Chorus 2

God will be your friend.
God will be your friend.
Jesus loves me and you. Yes, it's true
'Cause God, God will be your friend.

"I Will Be Your Friend" by Ben Glover and Jay Stocker.
© 2004 Group Publishing, Inc. All rights reserved.

What a Friend We Have in Jesus

Chorus

What a friend, what a friend we have!
What a friend, what a friend we have!

What a friend we have in Jesus,
All our sins and griefs to bear.
What a privilege to carry
Everything to God in prayer.

Oh, what peace we often forfeit,
Oh, what needless pain we bear,
All because we do not carry

Everything to God in prayer.

(Sing chorus.)

Have we trials and temptations?
Is there trouble anywhere?
We should never be discouraged;
Take it to the Lord in prayer.

Can we find a friend so faithful,
Who will all our sorrows share?
Jesus knows our every weakness;
Take it to the Lord in prayer.

(Sing chorus.)

"What a Friend We Have in Jesus" by Joseph Scriven and
Charles C. Converse.

We're a Circle of Friends

We're a circle of friends.
We've come together as one.
See the love never ends
'Cause we're friends with God's Son.
It's a circle of friends
With room for everyone,
And the fun never ends
'Cause we're a circle of friends!

Anyone who comes along,
This is where they belong.
In Jesus' name our love is strong.
So come on and shout this way cool song!

We're a circle of friends.
We've come together as one.
See the love never ends
'Cause we're friends with God's Son.
It's a circle of friends
With room for everyone,
And the fun never ends
'Cause we're a circle of friends!

"We're a Circle of Friends" by Dean-o.

"With All Your Heart" (Proverbs 3:5-6) by Jay Stocker.
© 2004 Group Publishing, Inc. All rights reserved.

With All Your Heart

(Proverbs 3:5-6)

Trust in the Lord with all your heart;
Do not depend on your own understanding.
Seek his will in all you do,
And he will direct, he will direct your path.

Trust in the Lord with all your heart;
Do not depend on your own understanding.
Seek his will in all you do,
And he will direct, he will direct your path.

Bridge

We need God's help.
We need to pray
So he will show us the way.

Trust in the Lord with all your heart;
Do not depend on your own understanding.
Seek his will in all you do,
And he will direct, he will direct your path.

Trust in the Lord with all your heart;
Do not depend on your own understanding.
Seek his will in all you do,
And he will direct, he will direct your path.

We Will Live Forever

(John 3:16)

Verse

For God so loved the world
That he gave his only Son,
So that everyone who believes in him will not perish.

For God so loved the world
That he gave his only Son,
So that everyone who believes in him will not perish.

Chorus

We will live, we will live forever (because of Jesus)!
We will live, we will live forever (because of Jesus)!

Verse

For God so loved the world
That he gave his only Son,
So that everyone who believes in him will not perish.

For God so loved the world
That he gave his only Son,
So that everyone who believes in him will not perish.

Chorus

We will live, we will live forever (because of Jesus)!
We will live, we will live forever (because of Jesus)!
We will live, we will live forever (because of Jesus)!
We will live, we will live forever (because of Jesus)!
We will live, we will live forever (because of Jesus)!
We will live, we will live forever (because of Jesus)!

Must Be Done in Love

Hey!

God, help me remember
What I need to do.
Help me serve others
In everything I do,
When I'm walking,
When I'm running,
When I'm standing,
Or when I am jumping.

Every step I take,
Every move I make,
It must be done in love.
Everything I say,
Everything I do,
It must be done in love.
Yeah, it must be done in love.
Must be done in love!
Hey!

God help me remember
What I need to do.
Help me serve others
In everything I do.
When I'm walking,
When I'm running,
When I'm standing,
Or when I am jumping.

Every step I take,
Every move I make,
It must be done in love.
Everything I say,
Everything I do,
It must be done in love,
Yeah, it must be done in love.
Oh, it must be done in love,
Must be done in love! Hey!

Standing on the Promises

Standing on the promises of Christ, my King,
Thro' eternal ages, let his praises ring.
"Glory in the highest," I will shout and sing,
Standing on the promises of God.

Standing, standing,
Standing on the promises of God, my Savior;
Standing, standing,
Standing on the promises of God.

Praise Him

Praise him; praise him.
Praise him in the morning;
Praise him in the noontime.
Praise him; praise him.
Praise him when the sun goes down.

Love him; love him.
Love him in the morning;
Love him in the noontime.
Love him; love him.
Love him when the sun goes down.

Serve him; serve him.
Serve him in the morning;
Serve him in the noontime.
Serve him; serve him.

Serve him when the sun goes down.

Jesus, Jesus

Jesus came and (clap) lived among us.
Now we can live for him.
Jesus came and (clap) walked among us.
Now we can walk with him.
Then he gave his life,
The greatest sacrifice!

Chorus

Jesus, Jesus, (clap)
Precious Jesus,
He died and rose again!
Jesus, Jesus, (clap)
Precious Jesus,
He gave his life for you and me!

Jesus came and (clap) lived among us.
Now we can live for him.
Jesus came and (clap) walked among us.
Now we can walk with him.
Then he gave his life,
The greatest sacrifice!

Chorus

Jesus, Jesus, (clap)
Precious Jesus,
He died and rose again!
Jesus, Jesus, (clap)
Precious Jesus,
He gave his life for you and me!

Jesus, Jesus, (clap)
Precious Jesus,
He died and rose again!
Jesus, Jesus, (clap)
Precious Jesus,
He gave his life for you and me!
He gave his life for you and me!
He gave his life for you and me!

"Jesus, Jesus" by Jay Stocker. © 2005 Group Publishing, Inc.
All rights reserved.

Your Friend

There's a need in every one of us—
It's written in the code of who we are—
To know and love each other
With a love that only comes from God's own heart.
There's so much for you and me
When it's Jesus who we see.

I will be your friend
Because the Lord has shown us
A love that never ends,
A bond that can't be broken.

You can count on me.
Whatever you need,
I will be here for you.
No matter where or when,
I will be your friend.

(Repeat.)

"Your Friend" by Jay Stocker. © 2005 Group Publishing, Inc.
All rights reserved.

Our Forever Friend

(Moose Mountain Theme Song)

Come on, everyone, let's gather around.

Verse

Here we are together again.
We're hangin' out with Jesus, our best friend!
He shows us how to live and love;
Now together we can have some fun!

He's our forever friend,
Forever friend.
Together forever…and forever never ends!
He walks right beside us wherever we go.
Yeah, we can count on Jesus,
Our forever friend, our forever friend!
Oh, he's forever.

(Repeat verse.)

He's our forever friend,
Forever friend.
Together forever…and forever never ends!
He walks right beside us wherever we go.
Yeah, we can count on Jesus,
Our forever friend, our forever friend!
Let's sing this one more time.
Here we go! Yeah!

He's our forever friend,
Forever friend.
Together forever…and forever never ends!
He walks right beside us wherever we go.
Yeah, we can count on Jesus,
Our forever friend, our forever friend!
Yeah, we can count on Jesus,
Our forever friend, our forever friend!

Oh, he's our friend.